Children and the State:
Whose Problem?

Edited by Jane Tunstill

CASSELL
London and New York

Cassell
Wellington House, 125 Strand, London WC2R 0BB
370 Lexington Avenue, New York, NY 10017–6550

First Published 1999

British Library Cataloguing-in-Publication Data
A catalogue record for this book is available from the British Library.

ISBN 0–304–70520–9 Hardback
    0–304–70521–7 Paperback

Library of Congress Cataloging-in-Publication Data
Children and the state, whose problem? / edited by Jane Tunstill.
    p.   cm.
    Includes bibliographical references and index.
    ISBN 0–304–70520–9. – ISBN 0–304–70521–7 (pbk.)
    1. Children–Government policy–Great Britain.   2. Child welfare–
Great Britain.   3. Children–Services for–Great Britain.
    4. Children–Legal status, laws, etc.–Great Britain.   I. Tunstill,
Jane.
    HV751.A6C588   1999
    362.7'0941–dc21   99–10515
                                                                                              CIP

Typeset by BookEns Ltd, Royston, Herts
Printed and bound in Great Britain by Bookcraft Ltd, Midsomer Norton

Contents

Contributors

Stewart Asquith is currently St Kentigern Professor for the Study of the Child at the Centre for the Child and Society at the University of Glasgow. He has held posts in the Scottish Office, and in both the Department of Criminology and the Department of Social Policy and Social Work at the University of Edinburgh; and was Stevenson Fellow in the Department of Social Policy and Social Work at the University of Glasgow. He has written widely on child-related issues and in particular on delinquency and juvenile justice with specific reference to the European context. For several years now he has undertaken consultancy and other projects for the Council of Europe on delinquency in Europe and juvenile justice in Central and Eastern Europe.

Crescy Cannan is Senior Lecturer in Social Policy and Social Work at the University of Sussex. She has a long-standing interest in comparative social policy and especially in social welfare policies in France and Germany in relation to children, youth and families. Her publications include *Changing Families, Changing Welfare: Family Centres and the Welfare State* (Harvester Wheatsheaf, 1992); with Lynne Berry and Karen Lyons, *Social Work and Europe* (BASW/Macmillan, 1992); and, as co-editor with Chris Warren, *Social Action for Children and Families: A Community Development Approach to Child and Family Welfare* (Routledge, 1997).

Elizabeth Cutting was a Research Associate in the Centre for the Child and Society at the University of Glasgow where she worked on a number of topics related to children who commit crime and the responses of state agencies to the behaviour of such children. She is currently working as a project manager for Save the Children Fund UK and is based in Edinburgh.

Sally Holtermann is an independent economist who specializes in the application of economies to social issues. She has written on child care and women's employment, equal opportunities, the labour market effects of the benefit system, and the impact of economic policies on children. Her recent publications include *Investing in Children: A Reassessment of the Cost of an Education and Day Care Service* (National Children's Bureau, 1995), *All Our Futures: The Impact of Public Expenditure and Fiscal Policies on Britain's Children and Young People* (Barnardo's, 1995) and *Weighing It Up: Applying Economic Evaluations to Social Welfare Programmes* (Joseph Rowntree Foundation, 1998).

Zarrina Kurtz is a consultant in Public Health and Health Policy. She worked as a paediatrician and general practitioner before further specialization in epidemiology and social medicine. She was formerly medical adviser to the Inner London Education Authority, senior lecturer at the Institute of Child Health, London, and Regional Consultant in Public Health in South Thames Regional Health Authority. Her academic, research and service career has focused on chronic illness in children and young people. She is currently leading a programme of national research on services for the mental health of children and young people, funded by the Department of Health. She is Honorary Adviser in Child Health to the National Children's Bureau.

Margaret Maden is Professor of Education and Director of the Centre for Successful Schools at Keele University. Previously she was Chief Education Officer in Warwickshire, and during this period was a member of the National Commission on Education (established by Sir Claus Moser in 1991). She has also been a headteacher in an inner London comprehensive school and geography teacher in a Brixton school. She is a council member of the Policy Studies Institute and an assessor for both the Organisation for Economic Co-operation and Development and the Harkness Foundation.

Peter Newell is co-ordinator of EPOCH (the campaign to end the physical punishment of children). He chairs the Council of the Children's Rights Development Unit (an independent project set up in 1992 to encourage full implementation of the UN Convention on the Rights of the Child in the UK), was a member and research co-ordinator of the Gulbenkian Foundation Commission on Children and Violence, and is a member of the Council for Disabled Children. Previously he was Director of the Advisory Centre for Education, and worked at the Children's Legal Centre. He has published widely on children's rights and child protection in the UK and abroad.

Kwame Owusu-Bempah is Lecturer in Psychology at the University of Leicester School of Social Work and Visiting Professor at the University of Babes-Bolyai, Romania. Professionally he is a chartered psychologist, registered nurse for the mentally handicapped, and qualified educator of adults. He has published extensively in both academic and professional areas. His major publications include 'Race, self-identity and social work', 'Racism of psychology: time for change' and *Professional Abuse of Black Childhood* (School of Social Work, Leicester University). His current research interests include the psychosocial development of children in lone-parent families (with Dennis Howitt).

Mary Ryan is a solicitor with considerable experience of family and child care law. She worked for the Family Rights Group for fifteen years, initially as Legal Adviser and then as Director. She now works as a freelance consultant and trainer on issues of child care law and social work policy and practice.

Jane Tunstill is Professor of Social Work at Royal Holloway, University of London, having previously held the Chair of Social Work Studies at Keele University. Her social work career includes working as a house-mother in a Girls Approved School and as Child Care Officer and Social Services social worker before she moved into social work education and research in the universities of Surrey, Leicester and East Anglia. She was Policy Advisor to the National Council of Voluntary Child Care Organisations for five years and is an Expert Member of the Registered Homes Tribunal. Her research includes child sexual abuse investigation, the impact of the Children Act 1989 on voluntary child care organizations, and most recently (with Jane Aldgate) two studies on Children in Need commissioned by the Department of Health. She is currently undertaking, also for the Department of Health, a National Study of Family Centres and a study for NSPCC of Family Support.

Introduction

Future social historians may find a certain irony in the absence of a Minister for Children in late twentieth-century Britain, given the concern of so many social policy initiatives with the relationship between children and young people with society and its institutions. However, while that perennially favourite subtitle *state, family and child* has usually been taken to mean the impact of the first of these on the third, in the closing years of the century this 'paternalistic' assumption would be undermined by the tenor of prevailing 'child-focused' proposals in most areas of government activity. Indeed, the incumbent of such a post, were it to exist, might well find herself or himself calling for a *reduction* of governmental interest in children on the grounds that a distinct watershed, if not a crisis, has emerged in the relationship between British children and British society. To put the point crudely, there is an increasingly common perception among politicians and the media that children not only *face* the traditional problems and challenges involved in negotiating a role in society, but now, to an unprecedented degree, actually *cause* them.

The dichotomy between these two opposed images of reality is symbolized by the conflicting values and policy aspirations which can be identified in legislation. For example, in the same time frame that a sense of moral near-panic seems to pervade the debate about youth justice in the debates around the 1998 Crime and Disorder Act, other policy initiatives deriving from the Children Act 1989 stress the necessity for a more integrated and multidisciplinary approach to the rights, needs and requirements of young people. At the same time as wageless and homeless young people face mounting political and media hostility, waged and accommodated young people are increasingly the target of commercial enterprise. In some areas children are seen as exerting rights as individuals, able to agree to or refuse medical treatment under the Children Act for example; in others they are seen as the recipient of services for them by their parents under the Education Reform Act. There is, however, a common theme running through many aspects of current policy, and it concerns the tendency to perceive children and young people as problems to be solved:

> New Labour is certainly 'concerned' about children: they are to be bundled off to cheap child care so their parents can work; licked into shape by educational competition and constant testing even at primary level; their criminal tendencies are to be curbed by harsh punishments or by being forcibly kept in (often with abusive parents, whom they were escaping in the first place). Children feature in these policies as problems, to be solved. (Judith Williamson, *Guardian*, 20 December 1997)

At the very least the inconsistencies in society's political and moral attitudes towards its young complicate the task of planning, delivering and evaluating policy and practice for them; this is a serious problem for staff, within many disciplines, who work with children and young people, such as those in health, education and social services departments. They are simultaneously asked to work for the physical, intellectual and social welfare of children and young people; and yet, at the same time, the legislative and policy context, and the organizational constraints of their own agencies, mean that far from contributing to the answers, they find themselves and their organization constituting part, if not most, of the problem.

The subject matter of this book is therefore the social and economic policy of childhood in late twentieth-century Britain; and the extent to which it enables us to explore the nature of the contemporary relationship between children and the state. Even to begin to answer the question implicit in its title, 'who is challenging whom?', means we need to appraise government activity across the board in terms of its ability to impede as well as facilitate the welfare of children and young people. Hendrick (1997, p. 8) comments, 'social policy ... can be very revealing of the value placed upon children by "society"; parents, educationalists, health and welfare personnel, politicians, churchmen and assorted moralists'; current foreign, economic and social policy provide an unusually bright spotlight on this matter.

The present volume adds to several valuable recent accounts of childhood and the state, including those of Pilcher and Wagg (1996) Hill and Tisdall (1997), Gittins (1998) and Daniel and Ivatts (1998). Indeed, it might be said that where politicians go, social science academics cannot be far behind!

Pilcher and Wagg start from a theoretical perspective of social constructionism, and examine the impact of the New Right on a range of policy issues including education; social services, poverty, crime and sexual behaviour. In *Thatcher's Children* (1996, p. 3) these authors acknowledge the key role played by the New Right in the mounting debate about children and childhood in the 1980s and 1990s.... Despite the departure of Margaret Thatcher in 1990, few would dispute the continued reverberation of Thatcherism as an identifiable cluster of arguments and assumptions in British political culture in the 1990s ... the discourse of the New Right has continued to characterize the Conservative administrations of John Major.

Although Pilcher and Wagg could not have known the outcome of the general election on 1 May 1997, their theoretical mapping helps us understand the way in which political ideology is a key force in determining the way in which we understand childhood, so in some ways it is only a case of replacing the blue lens in our social binoculars with a very pale pink one, to go on using their insights to guide our way.

Hill and Tisdall also adopt a social constructionist perspective to explore the nature of childhood in late twentieth-century Britain, but they emphasize the need to listen to children's own account of their experiences, and conclude that 'children should be seen *and* heard', although they acknowledge the way in which academics as well as politicians are often an impediment to such an ideal state of affairs.

The present volume is published at a time when many of the debates identified by the previous authors have reached a climax in New Labour policies towards children and the family. A central assumption, and one which underpins both the scope and the contents of the following chapters, is that while for children and young people in late twentieth-century Britain, the breadth and the depth of state activity are on the increase, the outcomes of that increased activity may be less than positive. Individual chapters address very different themes, from the perspective of their authors, who are experts in their respective fields. The volume is divided into two parts, with the intention that the first part identifies the main components of the *context* of childhood in the current decade. The second part comprises more detailed accounts of the issues within a range of professional disciplines or agencies.

The first part of the book therefore comprises an overview of professional assumptions and policy approaches in four key areas: *the law*, by Mary Ryan; *race and culture*, by Kwame Owusu-Bempah; *the economy*, by Sally Holtermann; and *Europe*, by Cressy Cannan. In the second part, five authors explore the impact of policy developments, again in four key areas: *health* (Zarrina Kurtz), *education* (Margaret Maden), *social services* (Jane Tunstill), and *youth justice* (Stewart Asquith and Elizabeth Cutting), Peter Newell provides an overview of the problems posed by the current absence of a co-ordinated approach by central government to the welfare of children.

Each chapter reviews the design of current provision in the light of the ideological assumptions and research data which to a more or less explicit degree have shaped the current system. Where appropriate, the authors have suggested the ways in which existing provision might be improved. The hope of all ten contributors is that if we honestly confront the philosophical contradictions and the deficits within the current system, children in the twenty-first century may cease to be seen as the *problem* and be allowed to contribute to designing the *answer*.

References

Daniel, P. and Ivatts, J. (1998) *Children and Social Policy*. Basingstoke: Macmillan.

Gittins, D. (1998) *The Child in Question*. Basingstoke: Macmillan.

Hendrick, H. (1997) *Children, Childhood and English Society, 1880–1990*. Cambridge: Cambridge University Press.

Hill, M. and Tisdall, K. (1997) *Children and Society*. London: Longman.

Pilcher, J. and Wagg, S. (1996) *Thatcher's Children*. London: Falmer.

PART 1

The Legal, Social, Economic and European Contexts of Childhood

1

Children and the law

Mary Ryan

Introduction

Children and the law is a broad topic and many books have been written about it. This chapter simply looks briefly at some of the ways in which the law distinguishes children from adults and then considers the anomalies that continue to exist in relation to the representation of children in family proceedings, the issues surrounding the expression of a child's 'wishes and feelings', and some of the case decisions on a child's rights, or lack of rights, to give or withhold consent to medical treatment.

The Children Act 1989 defines a 'child' as 'a person under the age of eighteen' (s. 105 Children Act 1989). The law thus sets the parameters for who will be regarded as a child and recognizes, broadly speaking, that children should be treated differently to adults. There is an element of inflexibility in the way this is applied so that, for example, no person under the age of 18 can vote, or own property such as a house, or hold a tenancy. The development of the law reflects society's changing views, so in the last half of the twentieth century we have seen the age of majority reduced from 21 to 18 (s. 1 Family Law Reform Act 1969), and throughout the century many different pieces of legislation have responded to society's recognition that this is an area where an element of flexibility is necessary, by providing that older adolescents should themselves, while still technically children, be treated differently from younger children. Indeed, criminal law and employment law still make a distinction between children and young people, although the age range for each is different in the two different spheres of law. The result of the need for flexibility in the law relating to children is complexity, and a need for succinct publications such as *At What Age Can I?* (Children's Legal Centre, 1996).

The law also reflects uncertainties and tensions within society over our attitude to children: should we effectively treat 16- to 18-year-olds as adults? We should allow children to have a say in decisions affecting their lives but do we require parents, as well as the state and the courts, to take children's views into account? Do we allow children to determine what should happen to them or do adults have responsibilities to make decisions in the interests of the child? Do we specify an age at which children can make decisions or do we leave adults to make an assessment of the child's level of understanding? In the criminal system the welfare versus justice debate continues. Do we want to punish children who offend or help them, or both? Should we continue to distinguish 10- to 14- from 14- to 18-year-olds? Should child witnesses be dealt with differently as compared with adult witnesses and does this undermine justice for defendants in criminal proceedings?

Differential treatment of children and adults

The law, both civil and criminal, recognizes that children should be treated differently from adults, and it also recognizes that older children should be treated differently from younger children, either by setting specific age limits or by considering the level of a child's understanding. This is the case both with common law (the law developed through court decisions only and not governed by statute) and with Acts of Parliament. Thus with negligence claims, the courts recognize that individuals and institutions owe a higher duty of care to children than they do to adults (for example, to take steps to prevent children falling off a balcony) and similarly, if an action in negligence is brought against a child, the court will take into consideration the child's ability or otherwise to make a judgement about the likely effect of their actions and will not treat them as if they were an adult.

A number of statutes govern contract law, and the general rule here is that children, of whatever age, cannot enter into contracts. There are exceptions, and this area of the law is complex and in need of overhaul. Prohibition on children entering into contracts is linked to the fact that children are perceived to be under a 'disability' so far as the law is concerned and that children are not responsible for their debts until they reach 18. Behind the basic principle is a desire to protect children from being persuaded into contracts and to protect adults from finding that they cannot enforce a contract they have entered into with a child.

Legislation places restrictions on the employment of children. It does this by creating specific criminal offences in relation to the employment of children (Children and Young Persons Act 1933). Such legislation is linked to a certain extent to our view as a society that children should have an opportunity to be educated, hence the responsibility on local education authorities to enforce this legislation and some of the provisions in the legislation being linked to school-leaving age. The legislation distinguishes between children under 13, 13 to school-leaving age (children) and school-leaving age to 18-year-olds (young people). There is an absolute prohibition on under-13s working, and there are many restrictions on the employment of children (as defined by the legislation), but the Employment Act 1989 removed most of the restrictions on the employment of young people, in line with the general political thrust at that time to remove regulation designed to protect employees. There is evidence that in general this legislation is poorly enforced.

Education legislation distinguishes children from adults by requiring the parents of children aged 5 to 16 to ensure that their child receives 'efficient full-time education suitable to his age, ability and aptitude and to any special educational needs he may have, either by regular attendance at school or otherwise' (S. 36 Education Act 1944). The requirement that a child receive full-time education can be enforced by criminal proceedings being brought against the parents or by the child being made the subject of an application for an education supervision order under the Children Act 1989. Although education legislation affects all children of compulsory school age there is a noticeable lack of emphasis in the legislation on taking into account children's wishes and feelings.

The criminal law recognizes the distinction between children and adults in a number of ways. In addition, it is one of the most complex areas of law in distinguishing between children of different ages. There are specific offences relating to the physical maltreatment or neglect of children, not only by adults, but in some instances by anyone over the age of 16. It creates specific offences in relation to selling specific items to children such as tobacco, alcohol and weapons. Children are protected by the same range of specification of sexual offences that protects adults, but in addition there are some sexual offences which can only be committed against children. The complex rules that relate to possible defences against specific offences are in some cases linked to the age of the alleged victim, the best-known being the consent of a girl aged 16 or over to sexual intercourse.

In relation to children who commit offences there is a basic rule that no one under 10 can be convicted of an offence. Legislation distinguishes between children, aged 10 to 14, and young people aged 14 to 18. Until 1998 there was a rebuttable presumption that children aged 10 to 14 were incapable of forming the necessary intention to commit a criminal offence. Thus children could be convicted of an offence only if the prosecution could also show that at the time the offence was committed the child knew what they were doing was seriously wrong. This common law rule, or presumption, was overturned by legislation. In 1993 legislation had also overturned the presumption that boys under 14 could not commit rape, buggery or offences involving sexual intercourse.

Children and young people are dealt with in different courts from those dealing with adults, although children can be tried in adult courts in certain circumstances. The sentences available are limited. Until 1997 a custodial sentence could only be passed on a young person of 15 or over. Legislation now permits 12- to 15-year-olds to be sentenced to a limited period of detention. In both cases particular conditions apply and are different from those which apply to adults. In relation to sentencing there continues to be a vociferous debate reflecting strongly held and conflicting views within society about our approach to children and young people who commit offences. How do we (and should we or can we) incorporate within a youth justice system elements of punishment, reparation for victims, a welfare response to the offender's own needs, and attempts to reduce offending?

The Children and Young Persons Act 1969 was an interesting, but ultimately unsuccessful, attempt to bring children (10- to 14-year-olds) who offended out of the criminal justice system altogether and into the welfare system. The 1969 Act set out the grounds for bringing care proceedings in relation to children on the basis of neglect or maltreatment, but it also provided for care orders to be made as a result of children offending generally. It was intended that care or supervision orders would be the only orders available for 10- to 14-year-olds, but the Act was unsuccessful in achieving this because the relevant sections of it were never implemented. At the root of this failure was the continuing conflict within society about the most appropriate approach to juvenile offending. The Children Act 1989 successfully amalgamates the private and public law relating to children and some aspects of health legislation but has nothing to do with juvenile offending, highlighting the distinction we make between children we see as 'victims' and those we see as 'villains' (Packman *et al.*, 1986).

Child witnesses in criminal proceedings are treated differently to a certain extent. A child of any age can give evidence in criminal proceedings, but a child under 14 will give unsworn evidence. Children under 14 who are the victims of violent offences, or children under 17 who are the victims of sexual offences, may give their evidence by video recording. If they are required for cross-examination they will have to attend court but may be cross-examined by video link. Judges no longer have to warn juries about convicting a defendant on the basis of the uncorroborated evidence of a child, except in cases concerning sexual offences where the rule remains that juries must be warned against convicting on the uncorroborated evidence of the alleged victim, whether that is a child or an adult. This is also an area of much debate, particularly in relation to sexual offences against children. Many concerns about the treatment of children as witnesses in the criminal justice system apply equally to adults and children, but the particular vulnerability of children is recognized, hence the introduction of video recording and video links. There are those who argue that more far-reaching changes are necessary to make it possible for children to give evidence and to make the experience less traumatic for them, but against this are the arguments of those concerned to uphold the civil liberties of people accused of crimes.

Representation of children in court

Children are distinguished from adults in relation to court proceedings generally because they are regarded as being persons under a disability, and therefore must bring or defend proceedings through an adult, called a 'next friend' if the child is bringing proceedings, or a 'guardian *ad litem*' if the child is defending proceedings. This does not apply to criminal proceedings. Normally the child will act through their parents but the position is more complex in both public and private family law cases concerning children, where the state may be intervening because of parental maltreatment or neglect of a child or where the child may be in dispute with either or both parents, or wishes to express a distinct view from parents disputing the child's upbringing. The Children Act has formalized the representation of children in public law proceedings, but the distinction between public and private law proceedings, the anomalies that remain, and government's concern over the cost of child care proceedings have provided fertile ground for debate and discussion about the representation of children and how children can make their views and wishes known to adults, to local authorities and other institutions, and to the courts.

Let us deal first with the issue of the representation of children. Children are parties to all public law proceedings, and legislation and court rules provide that they should have a guardian *ad litem* appointed for them from a panel set up under the Act, and that the court or the guardian should appoint a solicitor to represent the child. In contrast, children are not parties to private law proceedings, and normally their views are ascertained by a court welfare officer, who sets these out in their report to the court. Children do have the right to seek the permission of the court to make an application for an order in private law, such as a residence or contact order (Section 10(8) Children Act 1989). They can do this directly by going to a solicitor themselves, provided the solicitor considers that the child has sufficient understanding to give instructions (Rule 9.2A (1) Family Proceedings Rules 1991). The court could take a view different from that of the solicitor and insist that the child act through a next friend, who in this case would be the Official Solicitor.

Similarly, it is possible for the court to agree to make a child a party to private law proceedings, for example in a dispute between the parents over the residence of the child concerned, but there is no provision for a guardian *ad litem* to be appointed from a public law guardian *ad litem* panel, so once again it would be the Official Solicitor who is appointed, or another suitable adult. In cases brought by the local education authority under the Children Act for an education supervision order, there is no power to appoint a guardian *ad litem* from one of the panels. In these proceedings children are represented by a solicitor alone, normally appointed for them by the court. In adoption proceedings, which are governed by the Adoption Act 1976 and the Adoption Rules 1984, the children who are the subject of the application are parties to the proceedings only if the application is dealt with by the High Court, and will not be parties in the county court or family proceedings court. Where the application is opposed, a guardian *ad litem* will be appointed from a panel, but the guardian's role is governed by the adoption court rules and is different from the role of a guardian in public law proceedings. Thus the child's wishes and feelings will be reported to the court through the guardian's report, but the child will have no separate representation.

The court rules setting out the duties of guardians *ad litem* and solicitors in public law cases specify that the guardian shall instruct the solicitor 'unless the solicitor considers having taken into account the views of the guardian ad litem ... that the child wishes to give instructions which conflict with those of the guardian ad litem and that [the child] is able, having regard to his understanding, to give such instructions on his own behalf' (Rule 4.12 Family Proceedings Rules 1991). In such a case the solicitor should take instructions directly from the child and represent them as they would an adult. No age limits are given, so the child is here dependent on having a solicitor who feels competent to assess the child's level of understanding and is prepared to represent the child and advocate on their behalf in accordance with their instructions. In contrast, for children who are represented by the Official Solicitor in wardship proceedings in the High Court or in private law proceedings, the roles of guardian *ad litem* and solicitor are merged, which means that if the child's views and wishes are in conflict with what the Official Solicitor considers to be in the interests of the child, whatever the age of the child, he or she does not have an independent representative to advocate on their behalf in court.

The representation of children in public law Children Act proceedings that combines the independent assessment of the case by a guardian *ad litem* with representation by a solicitor, is widely regarded among practitioners both in England and Wales and elsewhere as a good model for the representation of children. There are criticisms, which particularly concern the representation of older children, questioning whether solicitors are willing, or indeed able, to identify when children's wishes conflict with those of the guardian (Masson and Oakley, forthcoming). The system is, however, under threat because of government's concern over the cost of public law proceedings. Changes to the legal aid system may lead to a reduction in the separate representation of children, as opposed to its expansion into the area of private law.

Taking into account children's wishes and feelings

In all family proceedings under the Children Act, the courts have to regard the child's welfare as their paramount consideration and in doing so they have to take into account, among other things, the wishes and feelings of the child (ss. 1(1) and (3) Children Act 1989). Case decisions indicate that the weight to be attached to a child's wishes and feelings will vary depending on the age of the child and the subject matter of the application. It is clear that the court may override a child's views, even those of an older child, where it considers that adherence to the child's wishes would compromise their long-term welfare.

Local authorities have a duty to safeguard and promote the welfare of looked-after children (those children in care or accommodation) but do not have to regard their welfare as paramount (s. 22(3)). They also have a duty to find out and take into account the wishes and feelings of looked-after children, and those children they are proposing to look after, in addition to the wishes and feelings of the child's parents and others connected with the child (ss. 22(4) and (5)). In relation to the provision of accommodation under Section 20 of the 1989 Act, it is specifically provided that children of 16 or over may enter or stay in accommodation contrary to their parents' wishes, if that is what the child wants. (Section 20(11) Children Act 1989).

In England and Wales, parents are not required to take into account the wishes and feelings of their children, whereas the Children (Scotland) Act 1995 does require any person in the exercise of their parental responsibilities to have regard 'so far as practicable' to the views of the child, taking into account the child's age and maturity. Children over 12 are assumed to have sufficient maturity, and for younger children it will depend on the individual child and the nature of the decision being made (s. 6). It is not clear how a child could enforce this duty, but those who argue for an amendment to legislation in England and Wales along similar lines would argue that it is important for legislation to set out the clear principle that parents should take into account their children's views when making decisions that concern them.

Thus where there is a conflict between individuals over the upbringing of a child, or where the state has intervened in family life, the law recognizes that children's views and wishes should be ascertained and listened to regardless of age, but how much they are taken into account will be linked to the child's understanding. There remain many practical hurdles to children being able to express their wishes and feelings. Even where children are parties to proceedings and the court rules entitle them to attend the hearing, the judiciary have made it clear that they do not think it is appropriate for children to attend (Children Act Advisory Committee, Final Report, June 1997, p. 36). Children may feel that their views have not been adequately represented by a welfare officer in private law proceedings, but may be unaware of their right to apply to be joined as a party, or find it much too daunting a prospect. Children represented by the Official Solicitor, or by a solicitor who does not identify a clash of views between the child and the guardian, may well feel they have no one actively arguing for their wishes in court. Looked-after children may find it very difficult to express their wishes and feelings in child protection conferences, reviews and meetings, or to make or pursue a complaint about an aspect of their care. It is noticeable that education legislation is silent on the subject of children's wishes and feelings, which will become an issue only if proceedings for an education supervision order are brought under the Children Act 1989.

Consent to medical treatment

Linked to the question of legislation providing for children's wishes to be taken into account is the specific issue of consent to medical treatment. The Family Law Reform Act 1969 provides that the consent of a person of 16 or 17 to any surgical, medical or dental treatment is as effective as if they were 18 or over, and where a 16- or 17-year-old consents to treatment it is not necessary to obtain the consent of a parent or guardian. The legislation specifically refers to consenting to treatment rather than objecting to it, but the general view was that it put 16- and 17-year-olds in the same position in relation to both objecting and consenting as an adult.

The case of *Gillick* v. *West Norfolk and Wisbech Area Health Authority* ([1986] 1 AC 112) dealt with the position in relation to children under 16. The question at issue was whether a doctor could lawfully give a girl under 16 contraceptive advice and treatment without the knowledge or consent of her parents. The House of Lords decided that children under 16 could acquire capacity to give consent to treatment, provided they had sufficient understanding and intelligence to be capable of making up their own mind on the matter. The House of Lords envisaged a high level of understanding before a child could be deemed by a doctor to have achieved 'Gillick competence'. Different judgments by different Law Lords meant that there remained some confusion over whether a doctor could act on the Gillick competent child's consent without any attempt to consult with the child's parents, but the general understanding of the case was that a child under 16 of sufficient understanding could object or consent to medical treatment in the same way as an adult could. This

'Gillick principle' was expressed in the Children Act 1989 in those parts which allow children, if they are of a sufficient understanding, to refuse to submit to medical or psychiatric examination or treatment ordered by the court.

Subsequently, court decisions have raised doubts not only about the rights of under-16s to give or withhold consent to medical treatment, but also about those of 16- and 17-year-olds. One case questioned whether the Gillick principle applied to psychiatric assessment in the same way that it applied to medical assessment (*R.* v *Waltham Forest ex parte G* [1989] 2 FLR 138). In the case of *Re R.* the Court of Appeal expressed the view that even where a child was competent to give consent, this did not mean that the parents lost their independent right to consent, and that the parent and the child would enjoy concurrent rights. The court then went on to say that this principle would apply to 16- and 17-year-olds as well, notwithstanding the Family Law Reform Act. These views were reiterated in the case of *Re W.* The effect of this could be that a Gillick competent child, or a 16- or 17-year-old, could have their consent or refusal to medical treatment overridden by their parents. In addition, both the above cases confirmed previous decisions that the court has the power to override a competent child's refusal and consent to treatment (*Re R. (Wardship: Medical Treatment)* [1992] 1 FLR 190; *Re W (Medical Treatment: Courts Jurisdiction)* [1992] 3 WLR 758).

International and European frameworks

The new Human Rights Act 1998 (due to come into force during the course of 2000) incorporates the European Convention into UK law, which will mean that citizens can complain of a breach in human rights to the domestic courts. All public authorities must comply with the rights of the convention incorporated in the Act. Where there is conflict between the convention and domestic statute law the matter will be referred to parliament. The Act introduces for the first time in UK law the notion of fundamental rights and will make the process of complaining about a breach of human rights much more straightforward than it has been.

The United Nations Convention on the Rights of the Child 1989 is not enforceable through domestic or international courts. In some of the states which have ratified the convention its provisions are automatically incorporated into domestic legislation but that is not the case in the UK. The view of the UK government is that the convention is consistent with existing legislation. Section 2 of the Human Rights Act 1998 leaves open the possibility of citing rights from other conventions (such as this one) on issues where the European convention is silent. This raises the possibility of these rights becoming enforceable.

The convention sets a useful framework for issues relating to children. The Committee on the Rights of the Child, set up under the convention, produces periodic reports on the operation of the convention. The states that have ratified the convention have to produce reports to the committee on the steps they have taken to ensure that the rights in the convention are given effect. These reports, and the committee's response to them, are public documents, and the committee can make suggestions and recommendations to the individual states about the steps they should take to ensure that the rights set out in the convention are protected. The treatment of children in the British youth justice system and the limited opportunities for children to make their views known and have them taken into account have been among the issues for which the UK has been criticized by the committee. (See Chapter 9, pp. 166–7.)

All aspects of children's lives, as with adults, are affected by legislation and the common law. The law indicates that as a society we consider that children should be protected from harm, neglect and maltreatment by parents and other adult carers; that they should be protected from exploitation by adults as employers; that they should be protected from products available to adults, such as alcohol, tobacco, weapons; that they should receive education; that in family proceedings, or when the state intervenes in family life, the child's welfare is paramount and the child's wishes and feelings should be taken into account; and in relation to youth justice there is an acknowledgement that children should be treated differently from adults. In the twenty-first century many debates will remain about how we will enable children to express their views and how we will take those views into account; about how we should approach youth justice; about how best to distinguish adolescents from younger children. We will also continue to debate whether as a society the UK takes sufficient account of the impact on children's lives of changes to legislation in areas such as state benefits, legal aid and housing, as well as in those areas specifically focused on children such as youth justice, family law, education provision and social services.

References

Children's Legal Centre (1996) *At What Age Can I?* London: CLC.

Masson, J. and Oakley, M. (forthcoming) *Out of Hearing: The Representation of Children by Guardians Ad litem and Solicitors in Public Law Proceedings.*

Packman, J., Randall, J. and Jacques, N. (1986) *Who Needs Care? Social Work Decisions about Children*, Oxford: Blackwell.

2

Race, culture and the child

Kwame Owusu-Bempah

Introduction

> To be born into an ethnic minority in Britain – particularly ... whose origins
> are in Bangladesh, the Caribbean or Pakistan – is to face a higher risk of
> leading a life marked by low income, repeated unemployment, poor health and
> housing ... than someone who is white. (Amin and Oppenheim, 1993, p. 63)

That British society is both racially and culturally heterogeneous is
publicly acknowledged, as a fact enshrined in a variety of legislation (Race
Relations Act 1976, Children Act 1989, and NHS and Community Care
Act 1990). The challenge in the approaching century is how we build on
that acknowledgement; whether we are prepared to formulate policies and
design procedures to ensure the provision of services appropriate to such a
society; whether we are prepared to ensure that, regardless of race or
ethnicity, all children have an equal chance of achieving their potential.
    Britain has historically been a multicultural nation, originally Welsh,
Scottish, Irish and English cultures, European (Western and Eastern)
cultures, and regional and class cultures. The issue now, therefore, is not
culture or ethnicity *per se*, but rather the cultures or cultural practices of
groups who are perceived by the majority group to be racially different –
people who are not white Caucasian. The following discussion highlights
some of the important issues about race and culture, and their
implications for policy and practice with ethnic minority children in
today's (and tomorrow's) Britain, children of racial and/or cultural
backgrounds perceived by the national majority as different.

Race

What, then, is race? Many, including policy-makers and practitioners,
now recognize race as socially fabricated; they accept that race is a social

and political entity with no scientific basis, a fallacy. Not only does race lack a scientific basis, but even the artificial divisions between the so-called racial groups are nebulous and unstable, shifting according to the prevailing social or political wind (Davis, 1991; Dummett, 1984; Howitt and Owusu-Bempah, 1994; Owusu-Bempah, 1997). Nevertheless, the quest for the notion of race and its meaning continues. This is mainly because race is a social construction that best serves the interests of those who designed it (Howitt, 1991). It provides a rationale or justification for policies and practices which advantage some and disadvantage others; it enables its inventors to justify their control over others, to rationalize their monopoly over power and resources. In short, it enables the acceptance of the otherwise unacceptable. As Appiah (1985) adroitly puts it, it is because 'there is nothing [else] in the world that can do all we ask "race" to do for us' (pp. 35–6). He points out, however, that 'What we miss through our obsession with [race] ... is, simply, reality' (pp. 35–6).

Reality in the present context, the reality facing us, is that race implies more than anatomy; it has acquired social significance beyond anything imaginable. Race implies not just a superior–inferior dichotomy (as many believe), but rather a 'trichotomy', distinctions between socially superior, not-so-superior and inferior groups. It serves as a cue to more significant attributes of a group, including its culture, whereby one group's culture is presumed to be superior (or not-so-inferior) to those of others. The discourse and rhetoric employed to identify and describe different racial groups and their worth have changed substantially over time; but the notion of race as a vital social reality endures. In other words, we seem to have difficulty in abandoning our belief in race because it is fabricated specifically to justify, or assuage our conscience about, our differential and unfair treatment of groups on the grounds of their skin colour.

The idea that racial classification determines the perception and treatment of people is an idea that spans several centuries, and one for which there is more than ample historical and contemporary evidence for both real and artificial groups (Esmail and Everington, 1993; Howitt and Owusu-Bempah, 1990; Owusu-Bempah, 1994; Richards, 1995). Owusu-Bempah (1994) and Richards (1995), for example, provide empirical demonstration of the continuing influence of the myth of race on the thinking and practice of professionals, such as social workers and nurses. Such research evidence is unsurprising, given that a profession's guiding principles, values and practice are largely influenced by prevailing societal values, beliefs, myths and folklore. Racial myths and stereotypes still pervade British society. In other words, in their dealings with ethnic minority children and families, for example, professionals have a long tradition of using race as a frame of reference. Thus, practitioners' perceptions, assessments and treatment of black or ethnic minority clients have been adversely affected or clouded by (mis)conceptions of race.

There is contemporary evidence indicating that professionals have a repertoire of beliefs and assumptions about ethnic minorities and their cultural practices, especially their child-rearing practices, which adversely affect their work with ethnic minority children (e.g., Owusu-Bempah, 1994; Richards, 1995). This is in spite of the fact that many professionals today avoid the term 'race'. Although they try to distance themselves from 'race', they still use it as a mutable concept, a concept which alters, fluctuates and adapts to the prevailing sociopolitical environment. For instance, the term 'culture' or 'ethnicity' is often employed euphemistically by politically correct professionals to signify the more contentious term 'race' or 'racial', to denote 'black', (with all its negative or, at best, exotic connotations). For example, Maitra (1996) has noted that, the children of immigrants from Western and Eastern European countries quickly tend to lose their ethnic or cultural minority status, while second- or even third-generation South Asians, Africans and African–Caribbeans remain ethnic minorities. They are perceived by professionals as out-groups and expected to be like 'us' in order to receive appropriate services, be they education, health care or even justice.

Culture

Any meaningful professional intervention should be guided not only by clients' needs, but also by their cultural beliefs and values. The 1989 Children Act actively encourages workers to 'include the wider family and friends in situations where shared care of children is the cultural "norm"'. Besides, many recognize that attention to the cultural context of children's environment and experiences (including their child-rearing experiences) is necessary in order to provide appropriate services (Boushel, 1994). Yet social workers still fail to appreciate, for example, the African adage 'It takes a whole village to raise a child.' They fail to accept the fact that adoption and fostering within the extended family or the larger community is a characteristic of sub-Saharan African cultures. This failure or reluctance continues to cause difficulties for both workers and their African clients, especially regarding private/informal fostering among students. Similarly, Maitra (1996) has observed that with ethnic minority children, professionals often require parenting assessments when the cause of the conflict appears to be parental authority, the parents' insistence on traditional practice. Professionals tend to disregard the fact that such family conflict is a common feature of all families, irrespective of culture. That is, family conflict assumes greater salience or significance for professionals when it involves ethnic minority families.

The tendency of many professionals to overreact to or misconstrue ethnic minority cultural practices may be due to a lack of understanding or respect for ethnic minority cultures. Culture, in its true sense, is more or less a composite structure of beliefs, mythology, religion, ideas, sentiments, institutions and objects internalized in varying degrees by its members, and which guides and regulates their thoughts and conduct. The culture of a given group is the sum of the shared ways of thought, reactions, rituals, customs, habits and behaviour acquired directly or vicariously by its members. It includes child-rearing practices, kinship patterns, marriage rites, diet, dress, music and art. Except for artefacts, most of the elements of a culture are intangible. They are things which its members carry in their minds and as such are a potent or motivational force in moulding and shaping their dreams, aspirations and conduct – their personality. In short, one's cultural background is inseparable from one's psychological processes.

Culture and the child

In terms of child-rearing practices or child care, we derive our meaning and understanding of childhood from our culture. Thus, how a group perceives childhood and, hence, brings up its children is determined by the group's culture. This evidently gives rise to cultural variations in the meaning of childhood and child-rearing practices. For example, in 'individualistic' cultures, such as Britain's, a high premium is placed upon loyalties to the 'self' (oneself), so that children in these societies are brought up to be individualistic. In these cultures, children are taught to see themselves as autonomous, distinct agents, immune from situational or environmental control; the child is socialized to conceive the 'self' as all-important and relatively omnipotent. By contrast, many other societies are collectivistic, in that they place a great emphasis upon group loyalties. Children are, therefore, socialized to see themselves in terms of their relation to both the physical and the social environments, to relate interdependently or coexist with their environment (Landrine, 1992; Marsella *et al.*, 1985; Owusu-Bempah, 1998; Owusu-Bempah and Howitt, 1995, 1997; Triandis, 1986). Members of these cultures feel psychologically empty or incomplete without a sense of belonging to the family and the community. This characteristic is manifest even in second-generation members of these cultures living in countries whose societies are characterized by individualism, such as Britain (van den Heuvel *et al.*, 1992; Marsella *et al.*, 1985; Owusu-Bempah, 1998).

For example, a study carried out on behalf of the Joseph Rowntree Foundation (Hyton, 1997) suggests that ethnic minority (or collectivistic) individuals who develop values which oppose the materialism and individualism of the UK majority community cope better with most social and personal problems. In this study, it was found that ethnic minority families preferred solving problems for themselves to voluntary agency or statutory solutions. Indeed, most of the ethnic minority respondents expressed concern about the actions of professionals, such as school-teachers and social workers. They saw them as interfering in and undermining parental authority. It was also found that a majority of the ethnic minority women interviewed were adapting to life in the UK, but preferred to stay within their own cultural traditions. These findings reinforce the call by many (e.g., Owusu-Bempah, 1998; Silavwe, 1995) for caution in the application of Western principles and values in cross-cultural social work with children and families.

It must be emphasized that even though most of Britain's ethnic minority communities may be described as collectivistic, each has identifying characteristics. Culturally, they differ in many important features, including child-rearing practices. These variations, in turn, differ from the majority culture, which is often placed above that of the ethnic minorities. Consequently, professionals tend to misinterpret and patho-logize minority cultural beliefs and habits, including their meanings of childhood and child-rearing practices. For example, South Asian children, especially girls, are typically viewed by professionals as overprotected, overcontrolled or oppressed by their families and their socialization process as whole. The obverse is believed about African–Caribbean children, that their families have no control over them, resulting in their 'delinquency – drug-taking, promiscuity, educational underachievement and criminality'. Paralogistically, these very same professionals seem to recommend the practices of each group for the other. They advise South Asian families to be lax in their socialization of children: 'the social worker I had ... prior to my son was taken into care ... said the child should not be taught, he should be allowed to go out and play and that's how they learn' (Howitt, 1992, p. 165). African–Caribbean families, on the other hand, are advised to restrict and control their children.

Psychologically, much of the (unconscious) professional urge to influence ethnic minority children and families to toe the majority cultural line stems from the assumption that they would be 'better off' if they experienced themselves and the world as Westerners, as the professionals themselves do. There seems to be a long tradition of this urge among those concerned with child welfare. For example, Wagner (1979) remarked of Dr Barnardo: 'he was fighting to retain custody, not principally to prevent children returning to cruel parents, but to prevent their being brought up as Roman Catholics (quoted by Forsythe, 1995, p. 7).

This is not to suggest that negative aspects of an ethnic minority family should be accepted as normal and used as an excuse for a non-intervention stance when a child desperately needs intervention and protection. Simple adherence to banal 'ethno-sensitivity' (sensitivity to ethnic minority cultures) may assume, for example, that abuse (seen as such even by members) is acceptable in the child's culture. The consequences of such oversensitivity may be no less harmful than insensitivity.

In essence, no group's culture is superior or inferior to that of another (Montagu, 1974). The differences observed between cultural groups are due to the simple fact that each group lives in a different physical and/or social environment:

> Thus, although the caretakers of young children do have goals that are universal (e.g., protection, socialisation), there are societal differences in the behaviours of caretakers that are related to the community's ecology, basic economy, social organisation, and value systems. (Whiting and Edwards, 1988, p. 89)

This means that there is no justification for professional concern about the adverse psychological effects of another cultural group's child-rearing practices. A recent British study (Hackett and Hackett, 1994) supports this view. The study was conducted in Manchester, and involved 100 Gujarati mothers and 100 indigenous white mothers. It examined the differences in child-rearing practices between the two groups. Specific areas of interest were discipline, feeding, sleeping arrangements and toilet training. The investigators found marked differences in all these areas. In the area of discipline, for example, they found similarities in the use of smacking and withholding privileges. However, the Gujarati mothers, compared to their white counterparts, preferred emotional methods of discipline, such as threats to send the child away (for misbehaviour), to withhdraw love and affection from the child, or to bring in an outside authority-figure, for example a teacher, doctor, social worker or police officer.

The Gujarati mothers' tactics of child discipline may be at odds with Western received wisdom. That is, many child care professionals, such as social workers trained in the Rogerian, Bowlbian or Ericksonian tradition, are likely to disapprove of these methods. However, it must be noted that the Gujarati children involved in the study were found to be emotionally better adjusted than their white counterparts. Hackett and Hackett's study clearly cautions against ethnocentrism, or 'professiono-centrism', the belief or assumption that, in the professional–client encounter, professional values are the only values; the belief that there is only one opinion, professional opinion; the assumption that the professional text is the sacred text (or the only knowledge-base); in short, the professional arrogance that the practitioner always knows best what is in the client's interest.

To be fair, it must be acknowledged that in recent years, partly as a result of pressures from ethnic minority communities, social workers and other professionals have made efforts to 'understand' Britain's ethnic minority cultures. Nevertheless, this by itself is not sufficient to enable them to meet the needs of ethnic minority children. To achieve this, they need also to respect their cultural backgrounds. Additionally, they must expand their knowledge of the social, political and economic causes of their clients' problems, while appreciating the role that they can play in helping or worsening those problems. The aim is to develop effective strategies to overcome the barriers to providing appropriate services to ethnic minority children and families.

The role of the research literature

Very often, discussions of this type tend to concentrate solely on practice and practitioners; usually, little is said about the source(s) of practitioners' knowledge-base regarding race and culture or ethnic minorities generally. Since practitioners derive their knowledge, including ideas about race, culture and ethnicity, largely from the academic and professional literature, we must discuss the role that writers and educators play in the creation and maintenance of the beliefs and assumptions held by practitioners and policy-makers about ethnic minority communities and their cultures and family structures. (See Howitt and Owusu-Bempah, 1994; Owusu-Bempah and Howitt, 1997, for detailed discussion.) To aid this discussion, we may use the portrayal of African–Caribbean children and families in the literature to typify some of the ways in which writers often present distorted and unfavourable images of ethnic minority children to practitioners, policy-makers, and the public at large.

Following a report published in the 1960s (Moynihan, 1965) concerning African-American families in the US (which purported to reveal 'a tangle of pathology') writers have continued to encourage practitioners, policy-makers and the public to see the African–Caribbean family structure – the keystone of any culture – as defective and problem-ridden. This picture has influenced all and sundry to construe African–Caribbean families as degenerative and dysfunctional, and to treat them accordingly. In Britain, examples of the objectification of the 'tangle of pathology' notion and its influence on social policy, and professional thinking and practice are to be found in the works even of those who should know better. These include such writers as Lobo (1978), Brian and Martin (1983), Dwivedi and Varma (1996) and Coleman (1994). For example, Lobo, a paediatrician of Indian origin, described African–Caribbean child-rearing practices in ways very similar to Moynihan's; for example, 'The curiously cold and unmotherly relationship between many West Indian mothers and their children has been noticed.... There is a distinct lack of warm, intimate, continuous relationship between the children and their mothers' (Lobo,

1978, p. 36). Perhaps because Lobo expected readers to accept these damaging claims about African–Caribbean child-rearing practices as self-evident, he deemed it unnecessary to provide any empirical evidence to support them. Instead, he presented them as social facts warranting further unsubstantiated assertions: 'these poor child-rearing practices are known to be able to cripple a child's development' (p. 37). He went further in providing professional child care workers with the *coup de grâce* for the African–Caribbean family, although in a seemingly understanding and sympathetic way, by describing the problems facing African–Caribbean children and families as a legacy of slavery times:

> The father in the West Indian culture is not the central, stable, providing person that he is in the Asian or European cultures. The loss of African child-rearing practices and their inadequate replacement by European practices are ascribed by most observers to the destructive effect of slavery. (p. 37)

Contained within this passage is a clear stereotype of the African–Caribbean father as irresponsible, absent or, missing, or where present, as someone who spends his welfare money on booze, drugs and gambling, while the best his neglected children can hope for is not to be beaten or abused in other ways. Furthermore, African–Caribbean mothers are held not to meet the standards of their European and Asian counterparts. Lobo's view is that the effects of the paucity of African–Caribbean parenting skills, and the African–Caribbean family as a whole, warrant only one comparison: 'the "maternal deprivation" effects of the West Indian child *living at home* is matched only by other children brought up in old-fashioned orphanage-institutions' (p. 37, emphasis added).

In the 1970s and early 1980s, this comparison would have hit a grating chord. At the time, child care professionals were increasingly anxious to de-institutionalize the care of children. Also, concerns about the problems of inner-city living had encouraged initiatives to provide alternative learning environments for pre-school children. Moreover, simple mother–infant physical contact (deemed essential for the healthy development of even monkeys) and continuity in a parent–child relationship, deemed vital by the then influential psychiatrist Bowlby (1951, 1969), are missing in the African–Caribbean family, according to Lobo's account. The consequences of such deprivation for the child's well-being were (and still are) believed to be detrimental: 'When deprived of maternal care, the child's development is almost always retarded – physically, intellectually and socially – and symptoms of physical and mental ill-health may appear' (Bowlby, 1951, p. 15). Thus, at the time, it would have been impossible to imagine a much worse environment for a child than Lobo's portrait of African–Caribbean families. It is impossible to assess the extent to which this picture of the African–Caribbean family has influenced, and continues to influence, the decisions of child care professionals (health visitors, teachers, social workers, school psychologists, child psychiatrists and therapists) concerning African–Caribbean families and children. Could the sentiments so clearly enunciated by Lobo be responsible, at least partly, for the often reported over-representation of black children in the public child care system? Lobo's views must not be seen as history. They are still being reproduced, in textbooks in one form or another and at the very end of the twentieth century, one still comes across them in students' written work. Students tend to accept them unquestioningly, owing mainly to the pseudo-scientific aura surrounding them.

Assertions of black family pathology are victim-blaming and serve only to convey the message that there is little, if anything, that can be done by policy-makers and professionals to improve the lot of African–Caribbean children and their families.

The web of influence of such writers as Lobo on the race thinking of professionals involved with black children is too complex to trace completely; one can only speculate. Nevertheless, there are numerous examples of its direct and indirect influence from research built on the assumptions of the 'black family pathology' thesis (Howitt, 1991; Owusu-Bempah, 1994, 1997). A further example of the ways in which writers reinforce the belief in the 'black family pathology' concerns an influential textbook for nursery nurses (Brian and Martin, 1983). Its authors, a teacher and a health visitor, chose to discuss black children specifically under the heading 'children with special needs'. They discuss the following categories of children under the same heading: premature babies, children with handicaps (whom they define as children 'whose development is impaired by disease or injury', p. 232), deprived and disadvantaged children, materially, environmentally and socially deprived children, and intellectually, culturally and educationally deprived and disadvantaged children.

Brian and Martin (1983) resort to myths about African–Caribbean families and their cultural practices, especially their child-rearing practices, when recommending ways of 'helping' their children. They draw special attention to the 'problems' of a lack of educational encouragement at home, and disciplinary problems presented by African–Caribbean children as a consequence of their upbringing. Regarding educational encouragement, they write, '[West Indian] children may need special guidance in handling and caring for play materials or books, as these are often lacking in their homes' (p. 246). When dealing with problems of discipline, Brian and Martin again resort to stereotypes concerning the children's 'lack of self-control' and 'sense of rhythm':

> They find a great deal of choice bewildering, as they are not encouraged to be self-regulating at home. Strict discipline and ... corporal punishment at home

can mean that softly-spoken restraints and explanations about behaviour limitations go unheeded at nursery... Their responsiveness to music makes it almost impossible for them to remain still when music is being played. (pp. 246–7)

Contrast this with the textbook's account of Chinese families and their children:

Young Chinese children may be involved in the family business ... because this is their culture – that *all* contribute to the family income ... business ... hours may not be compatible with ideal children's bedtimes, and in the nursery hours the children may appear fatigued... [Chinese] children are encouraged in the home to be docile and hard-working. Education is rated very highly. (p. 247, emphasis in the original)

The sympathetic understanding communicated to readers about the circumstances of Chinese families contrasts markedly with the way in which African–Caribbean families are accused of physical abuse of their children, and blamed also for the children's presumed inferior intellectual make-up, emotionality and lack of discipline. That Chinese children of nursery age supposedly 'contribute to the family income' seems to raise no concern for the authors.

At the very least, such textbook pronouncements do nothing to counter and challenge the racist attitudes, assumptions and stereotypes of the readers. Worse still, they may well cultivate and reinforce ideas hostile to the well-being of black children in the minds of students and practitioners dealing with ethnic minority children. Put crudely, the authors' message to nursery staff and school teachers is: be firm with African–Caribbean children; occupy them in a corner of the nursery or classroom with music; don't waste time and valuable resources trying to engage them intellectually. Brian and Martin encourage other practitioners to assume child physical abuse or neglect in African–Caribbean families, but, at the same time, encourage them to ignore the same behaviour (in the form of child labour) in Chinese families. The first edition of this textbook was published in 1980, the third appeared in 1989. Its long-term influence on child care professionals must be of concern to anyone involved in the care of ethnic minority children.

As a result of the proliferation of such writing and research, social workers, teachers, health workers and other professionals working with ethnic minority children can readily find (pseudo)evidence to support the view that these youngsters and their families are a problem, and to treat them accordingly. Some writers tend to encourage professionals and policy-makers to ignore the structural problems facing these children and their families, to seek the causes of their difficulties in their culture, especially their family structure.

Dwivedi and Varma (1996) continue to encourage child care professionals to do that. Writing in 1996, they give the following description of African–Caribbean families, and their children's developmental needs: 'West Indians [in Britain] tend to be unaware of the emotional needs of the growing child.... Many West Indian children now attending secondary schools are grossly retarded educationally' (pp. 43–4). Readers may judge for themselves whether it is ethically and professionally responsible to publish such material in a volume aimed at child care professionals of the next century. The same authors deliver a *coup de grâce* to the educational aspirations of African–Caribbean children in the following recommendation:

> We ... need to think in terms of planning, for the children ... the type of curriculum which would aim at exploiting their particular interests, with emphasis on ... woodwork, metalwork, handicraft, art.... For this group particularly we would need a reorganization of the traditional remedial class within the school, if we hope to sustain their interest in class, and reduce the degree of difficult behaviour seen at school. (Dwivedi and Varma, 1996, p. 47).

Coleman (1994) offers a new version of the 'black family pathology' thesis in which parenting skills are claimed to be harmed by parental migration. She argues that emigrant parents from the Caribbean temporarily left their children with grandparents. This hardly applies to the circumstances of most of the children she describes – young children of 'mixed-race' parentage, born in Britain. Nevertheless, according to her, this engendered resentment in the children towards their mother in particular. She also stresses the adverse inter-generational effects of this form of parental 'neglect': 'this, in turn, may inhibit healthy parenting on the part of the mother to her own child. A pattern of ambivalent and inconsistent parenting can therefore be established' (p. 5). The basis of this assertion is uncertain. Also noteworthy is the exclusion of the father in this scenario. Like other writers, Coleman reinforces the popular stereotype of the absent-father African–Caribbean family. She adds a further pillar to the black family pathology propaganda by highlighting informal adoption as yet another compounding factor in the difficulties facing black children in Britain.

The arguments put forward by the above authors all present versions of the Moynihan problem-approach to the study and understanding of black families – the stereotypic view that black families are intrinsically degenerative and pathologize their offspring. They disregard and encourage others to ignore other perspectives to the understanding of African–Caribbean and other ethnic minority families, and the difficult circumstances in which they live. Sadly, such literature, reinforced by the media and political propaganda, is seen by many as an authoritative confirmation of the popular belief that black families have problems which they can deal with only with the help of white professionals. Father absence, lone-parent mothers, matriarchal family structures, divorce, lackadaisical discipline and so forth are believed to typify the African–Caribbean family. The list for South Asian families is different, but equally long: overcrowded households, oppressive males and over-protection (or suffocation) of their children are a few of the 'pathological' features typically ascribed to them.

Black family strength

There are, of course, other perspectives to the study and understanding of ethnic minority families. Unlike the problem-family approach, these perspectives regard the structures of ethnic minority families as a means of dealing with a hostile social and economic environment. The structural-functional model, for example, stresses the positive, resilient and adaptive features of black and other ethnic minority families. This perspective sees the involvement of the extended family and the community, including informal fostering and adoption as a means of coping with poverty or establishing social networks (e.g. McAdoo, 1988; Littlejohn-Blake and Darling, 1993; Hyton, 1997).

In the US, Littlejohn-Blake and Darling (1993) reviewed studies concerning the strengths of the black American family. They suggest, among other things, that:

1. There is a religious and spiritual commitment in some black families which provides a purpose and orientation in life and faith that things will improve.
2. Black families are more capable of absorbing other people into the household. This is one of the mechanisms by which economic and moral assistance can be provided; informal adoption may provide a community social service in times of difficulty or in difficult circumstances. The informal network provides strength, stability and guidance within the community.
3. Black parents are ambitious for the economic and educational advancement of their children.
4. Children in black families develop pride and a strong sense of self- or personal identity including self-esteem as well as ethnic awareness.

The recent British study (Hyton, 1997) described previously reported similar findings.

As we have already seen, even helping professionals – for instance, social workers and nurses – problematize ethnic minority families and relate to them in ways which adversely affect them and their communities.

This happens in many areas of their work with the ethnic communities, including child protection. That ethnic minority families are inadequate families which fail or oppress their children frequently and dramatically is a dominant theme in the activities and beliefs of child care professionals. The commonly held assumptions that African–Caribbean youngsters manifest 'behavioural difficulties' or 'intellectual deficits', or that South Asian children, especially girls, are pathologically submissive owing to their 'oppressive' upbringing, mean that public provision for these children has been tailored accordingly, but catastrophically, for their welfare. Such views must be rejected when addressing the needs of ethnic minority children and their families.

Black professionals

As I have indicated already, even those whom one would expect to be more understanding or sympathetic towards ethnic minority children and families' circumstances sometimes propagate ideas or perspectives damaging to their well-being. This raises the pertinent question as to whether the recruitment of more ethnic minority professionals by itself will improve the situation for ethnic minority clients. Both British and North American studies suggest that this is not necessarily the case (e.g. Barth, 1997; Courtney *et al.*, 1996; O'Brian, 1990; Owusu-Bempah, 1989, 1990, 1994, 1997). Thus in the area of fostering and adoption, for example, Barth (1997) suggests (on the basis of research evidence) that the power of the ethnic matching preferences be reduced in the interests of the children: 'distasteful as this may be to many adoption specialists of all ethnic backgrounds, reducing the emphasis on racial matching must be a component of any serious plan to provide equal rights to a family for African-American children' (p. 302). Such views as this seriously question the usefulness of the notion of 'black perspectives', for instance in social work. Its utility is further questioned by its proponents' (e.g. Ahmad, 1990; Robinson, 1995) failure to define it. No group of workers, including social workers, can claim a professional status on the basis of ideas which cannot be defined. It appears, therefore, that this notion serves only to muddy the waters. To borrow Wakefield's (1996) suggestion in relation to ecosystems, 'black perspectives' proponents confuse the field's intellectual discourse by trying to force their ideological agenda on the profession. In practical terms, one cannot guarantee the effectiveness of a practice based upon fuzzy ideas, so that the claim that social workers need 'black perspectives' in order to ensure their effectiveness appears to be baseless. Indeed, Owusu-Bempah (1994, 1997) has argued that the only utility of such untested ideas as 'black perspectives', 'black culture', 'black identity', all of which derive from the notion of race (itself unfounded), is in further disadvantaging ethnic minority children (and adults) in the provision of services and facilities.

This is *by no means* to suggest that ethnic minority members have no part to play in the child welfare professions. The argument here is that, as far as helping ethnic minority children and families is concerned, their most valuable contribution would appear to be one of helping other colleagues to develop an understanding of, and respect for, ethnic minority cultures and cultural practices. Individually, they cannot claim expertise in all matters cultural. Many (e.g. Owusu-Bempah, 1990; Owusu-Bempah and Howitt, 1999; Stevenson, 1998) have warned against the temptation to use ethnic minority professionals to 'ghettoize' services to ethnic minority communities and their children.

Conclusion

 It goes without saying that provision for ethnic minority children must vary according to the child's individual requirements. No standard package is available which could be expected to meet the needs of all children. However, as a group, these children have a shared pool of needs or experiences which are distinct from those of children from the dominant culture. Their experiences of racism are among the most salient of these. Being on the receiving end of racial prejudice, abuse and discrimination is inevitably influential in ways which simply do not apply to other groups of children. Furthermore, research (Brown, 1984; Modood, 1997; Skellington and Morris, 1992) shows that racism is experienced by the significant people in their lives – parents, siblings, uncles, aunts and grandparents – in virtually every important sector of society.

The racial injustice experienced by their significant others is directly and vicariously experienced by children. It is quite easy to see how the inter-generational effects of racial disadvantage operate. For example, parents who were discriminated against in education are more likely to transmit negative feelings about schooling to their offspring; bad child care decisions made by professionals may cause both the parents and the children to suffer a sense of injustice; a child whose mother received inadequate or inappropriate antenatal care owing to the racism within the health care system may carry the effects for life; parents who have been allocated poor housing on racial grounds have little choice but to live in deleterious circumstances with their children. The list is endless. Dummett (1984) has described the process by which racism takes its toll as being a pattern rather than a simple accumulation of experiences: 'each instance of discrimination against you increases the likelihood of discrimination working against you in some other instance' (p. 134).

Addressing fully the needs of black children requires a recognition of, and solutions to, racism's injurious effects on them. Such solutions, however, will not be found without a genuine desire and a concerted political will to change. Furthermore, the necessary changes can be effected only if child care professionals and policy-makers have accurate information about ethnic minority children upon which to base decisions and practice. Racially and culturally unbiased messages in which there is no room for myths, assumptions, stereotypes and conjecture are crucial to this important task. None of this is outside our collective will or individual power: 'None is totally without power; all groups have ... and, therefore, the capacity to veto business as usual' (Willie, 1993, p. 454). The issue, then, is whether we are prepared to exercise our power in ways which will benefit ethnic minority children.

Obviously, the necessary changes require a new approach not only to practice and policy, but, more importantly, to professional education. In other words, to enable practitioners to be effective, and policy-makers to formulate the right policies, their education and training, including the literature which they are assigned, should be empowering. Their education should equip them with 'the means to critically appropriate knowledge existing outside their immediate experience in order to broaden their understanding of themselves, the world, and the possibilities for transforming the taken-for-granted assumptions about the way we live' (Spring, 1994, p. 27). In other words, as Spring suggests, practitioners are empowered to empower the powerless when those practitioners change their way of thinking, when they become aware that they can exercise political power to bring about changes in their social and economic conditions and those of their clients. In short, at the core of an empowering child care practice should be an untiring quest and burning desire to eliminate racial injustice, to promote the well-being of all children, regardless of their race, culture, ethnicity, creed, gender or class.

References

Ahmad, D. (1990) *Black Perspectives in Social Work*. Birmingham: Venture Press.

Amin, K. and Oppenheim, C. (1992) *Poverty in Black and White: Deprivation and Ethnic Minorities*. London: Child Poverty Action Group.

Appiah, K.A. (1985) The uncompleted argument: Du Bois and the illusion of race. In H.L. Gates, Jr (ed.), *'Race', Writing and Difference*, pp. 21–37. Chicago: University of Chicago Press.

Barth, R.P. (1997) Effects of age and race on the odds of adoption versus remaining in long-term out-of-home care. *Child Welfare*, 76 (2), 285–308.

Boushel, M. (1994) The protective environment of children: towards a framework for anti-oppressive, cross-cultural and cross-national understanding. *British Journal of Social Work*, 24, 173–90.

Bowlby, J. (1951) *Maternal Care and Mental Health*. Geneva: World Health Organization.

Bowlby, J. (1969) *Attachment and Loss*. London: Howarth Press.

Brian, J. and Martin, M.D. (1983) *Child Care and Health for Nursery Nurses*. Amersham: Hulton.

Brown, C. (1984) *Black and White Britain: The Third PI Survey*. Aldershot: Gower.

Coleman, J. (1994) Black children in care: crisis of identity. *Runnymede Bulletin*, October, 4-5.

Courtney, M., Barth, R.P., Berrick, J.D., Brooks, D., Needell, B. and Park, L. (1996) Race and child welfare services: past research and future directions. *Child Welfare*, 75, 99–137.

Davis, F.G. (1991) *Who Is Black? One Nation's Definition*. University Park: Pennsylvania State University Press.

Dummett, A. (1984) *A Portrait of English Racism*. London: CARAF Publications.

Dwivedi, K.N. and Varma, V.P. (eds) (1996) *Meeting the Needs of Ethnic Minority Children: A Handbook for Professionals*. London: Jessica Kingsley.

Esmail, A. and Everington, S. (1993) Racial discrimination against doctors from ethnic minorities. *British Medical Journal*, 306, 691–2.

Forsythe, B. (1995) Discrimination in social work: an historical note. *British Journal of Social Work*, 25, 1–16.

Hackett, L. and Hackett, R. (1994) Child-rearing practices and psychiatric disorder in Gujarati and British children. *British Journal of Social Work*. 24, 191–202.

Howitt, D. (1991) *Concerning Psychology: Psychology Applied to Social Issues*. Milton Keynes: Open University Press.

Howitt, D. (1992) *Child Abuse Errors: When Good Intentions Go Wrong*. Hemel Hempstead: Harvester Wheatsheaf.

Howitt, D. and Owusu-Bempah, J. (1990) Pragmatics of institutional racism: beyond words. *Human Relations*, 43, 885–9.

Howitt, D. and Owusu-Bempah, J. (1994) *The Racism of Psychology: Time for Change*. Hemel Hempstead: Harvester Wheatsheaf.

Hyton, C. (1997) *Black Families' Survival Strategies: Way of Coping in UK Society*. York: Joseph Rowntree Foundation.

Landrine, H. (1992) Clinical implications of cultural differences: the referential versus the indexical self. *Clinical Psychology Review*, 12, 401–15.

Littlejohn-Blake, S.M. and Darling, C.A. (1993) Understanding the strengths of African American families. *Journal of Black Studies*, 23 (4), 460–71.

Lobo, E. (1978) *Children of Immigrants to Britain: Their Health and Social Problems*. London: Allen and Unwin.

McAdoo, H.P. (1988) Transgenerational patterns of upward mobility in African American families. In H.P. McAdoo (ed.), *Black Families*, pp. 225–37 New York: Oxford University Press.

Maitra, B. (1996) Child abuse: a universal 'diagnostic' category? The implication of culture in definition and assessment. *International Journal of Social Psychiatry*, 42, 287–304.

Marsella, A.J., Devos, G. and Hsu, L.K. (1985) *Culture and Self: Asian and Western Perspectives*. New York: Tavistock

Modood, T. (1997) Qualifications and English language. In T. Modood, R. Berthoud, J. Lakey, J. Nazroo, P. Smith, S. Virdee and S. Beishon, *Ethnic Minorities in Britain: Diversity and Disadvantage*, pp. 60–82 London: Policy Studies Institute.

Montagu, A. (1974) *Man's Most Dangerous Myth: The Fallacy of Race*. New York: Oxford University Press.

Moynihan, D. (1965) *The Negro Family in The United States: the Case for Action*. Washington, DC: Government Printing Press.

O'Brian, C. (1990) Family therapy with black families. *Journal of Family Therapy*, 12, 3–16.

Owusu-Bempah, J. (1989) The new institutional racism. *Community Care*, 14 September, 23–5.

Owusu-Bempah, J. (1990) Toeing the white line. *Community Care*, 1 November, 16–17.

Owusu-Bempah, J. (1994) Race, self-identity and social work. *British Journal of Social Work*; 24, 123–36.

Owusu-Bempah, J. (1997) Race. In M. Davies (ed.), *The Blackwell Companion to Social Work*, pp. 50–6. Oxford: Blackwell.

Owusu-Bempah, J. (1998) The relevance of confidentiality in social work practice across cultures. In B.R. Compton and B. Gallaway (eds), *Social Work Processes*, pp. 151–70 6th edn. Pacific Grove, CA: Brooks/Cole.

Owusu-Bempah, J. and Howitt, D. (1995) How Eurocentric psychology damages Africa. *The Psychologist*, 18 (10), 462–5.

Owusu-Bempah, J. and Howitt, D. (1997) *Professional Abuse of Black Childhood*. Leicester: School of Social Work, University of Leicester.

Owusu-Bempah, K. and Howitt, D. (1999) Even their 'soul' is defective. *The Psychologist: Bulletin of the British Psychological Society*, 12 (3), 126–30.

Richards, K.D. (1995) *A Content Analysis of Texts in a Clinical Setting*. Birmingham: Aston University.

Robinson, L. (1995) *Psychology for Social Workers: Black Perspectives*. London: Routledge.

Silavwe, G.W. (1995) The need for a new social work perspective in an African setting: the case of social casework in Zambia. *British Journal of Social Work*, 25, 71–84

Skellington, R. and Morris, P. (1992) *Race in Britain Today.* London: Sage.

Spring, J. (1994) *Wheels in the Head: Educational Philosophies of Authority, Freedom, and Culture from Socrates to Paulo Freire.* New York: McGraw-Hill.

Stevenson, O. (1998) *Neglect: Issues and Dilemmas.* Oxford: Blackwell.

Triandis, H.C. (1986) Collectivism vs. individualism: a reconceptualization of a basic concept in cross-cultural psychology. In C. Bagley and K. Varma (eds), *Personality, Cognition and Values: Cross-Cultural Perspectives of Childhood and Adolescence.* London: Macmillan.

van den Heuvel, H., Heuval, H., Tellegen, G. and Koomen (1992) Cultural differences in the use of psychological and social characteristics in children's self-understanding. *European Journal of Social Psychology,* 22, 353–62.

Wakefield, J.C. (1996) Does social work need the eco-systems perspective? Part 1. Is the perspective clinically useful? *Social Service Review,* 70, 1–32.

Whiting, B.B. and Edwards, C.P. (1988) *Children of Different Worlds: The Formation of Social Behavior.* Cambridge, MA: Harvard University Press.

Willie, C.V. (1993) Social theory and social policy derived from the black family experience. *Journal of Black Studies,* 23, 451–9.

3

Children and the economy

Sally Holtermann

Children constitute over one fifth of the UK population. Out of the total public expenditure of £309 billion in 1996/97 (HM Treasury, 1997), a large part is accounted for by direct spending on children and young people: most of the £37 million education budget, all of children's personal social services, child benefit and one-parent benefit as well as child allowances in other social security benefits. As well, a large part of private spending is directly or indirectly devoted to children and their needs. Thus children have a major influence in shaping the national economy, and it might therefore be expected that they would have a major role in theoretical and empirical economics, and that there would be a substantial body of work analysing the impact of children on the economy, and conversely the impact of economic life on children. What is the reality?

Children and economic theory

Two types of economic decision-makers (households and firms) are usually distinguished in theoretical economics, and these are the basic units of analysis in microeconomics. Households consume goods and services and supply labour. Firms produce goods and services using inputs of labour and materials. Individuals enter either as one-person households, or, in refinements of the analysis of households, as agents within households each having his or her own pattern of consumption and labour supply. The decision about labour supply is sometimes divided into two elements: whether to participate in the labour market, and if so for how many hours.

Economic activities are usually treated as the result of decisions made to meet some objective (personal welfare (referred to as 'utility') in the case of households and profit in the case of firms) subject to constraints imposed by prices and incomes, personal circumstances, and the regulatory and legal framework of the day. The budget constraint is met when income is exactly equal to spending, which itself is the sum of the prices times the quantities of all the goods and services consumed, but departures from exactly fulfilling the budget constraint can be made through saving and borrowing.

Government policy is usually treated as incorporating additional constraints upon the actions of these economic agents, or altering the parameters in the economic equations they face in making decisions. Through indirect taxation the government influences the prices of commodities in the market place; through income tax and social security benefits it redistributes income from the well-off to the poor and influences the financial return from employment; and through interest rate policy it influences the price of borrowing and saving.

The basic theoretical model can be refined in various ways: by the introduction of broader considerations into the objectives of households and firms; by the inclusion of uncertainty about economic facts, external effects (unpriced side-effects of consumption or production decisions) and public goods (goods from which no consumer can be excluded), and so on. Social and psychological factors could be included, but usually only as exogenous variables (constant background factors). Nowadays all economic theory is developed through the medium of mathematics. Psychosocial phenomena that cannot be expressed quantitatively have a poor chance of being included as endogenous variables (changeable and explained within the theory).

Economic theory can provide a distinctive place for children in a variety of ways, each way reflecting some reality of the role of children in the economy. A fairly technical review of the American literature is provided by Browning (1992).

Children as economic agents

Many children and young people have their own independent source of income through pocket money and earnings and can make their own decisions about consumption and labour supply. The market sector recognizes the importance of children's purchasing power through regular surveys of pocket money. The government's family spending survey (Office for National Statistics, 1997b) shows that in 1995/96 children aged between 7 and 15 spent more than £50 million a week of their own money – £2.6 billion a year. A random sample survey found that children receive on average £250 at Christmas – £3 billion a year (Middleton et al., 1997).

Children could be treated within economic theory as independent economic agents, but although the role of children as consumers has been examined in empirical work, no branch of theoretical economics has been developed from this starting-point, possibly because, in theoretical terms, children would not be distinctively different from adults.

Influence of children on household economic behaviour

In contrast, however, there is a large body of economic theory, and associated empirical work, that gives children an indirect role in determining many of their parents' decisions about consumption and labour supply. For instance, it is routine in the statistical modelling of the demand for commodities to allow for some influence of children on the behaviour of the adults in the household through the addition of variables for the presence of children and their ages.

The presence of children is a key variable in models that explain labour market participation. In work emanating from Chicago in the 1960s (Becker, 1965), the traditional theory of household behaviour underwent significant development through recognition of the fact that parental budget constraints include both time and money. This innovation has spawned many extensions. Children can be incorporated, both through the time needed for their care and through consumption specifically for children.

Here children are treated as a personal circumstance of the adult and enter the economic calculus only through the preferences of their parents. This formulation in its simple form inadequately represents the experience of many parents, which frequently registers a discrepancy between their own preferences and those of their children. Parents are subject to pressures on their spending patterns to meet the wishes of their children, often when their own earning power may be diminished by a break from employment. They have to reconcile the conflicting pressures on their time and resources.

Models of household behaviour have been used particularly to underpin the statistical estimation of the effects of children on the labour supply of women, and to explain the well-known facts on the lower labour-market participation of women with young children. In some of these models the use of child care services while parents are at work is included as one of the consumption variables, and the price of child care enters the budget constraint and is assumed to work in effect like a tax on wages. Empirical estimations of some of these models have calculated large responses of women's employment to the cost of child care (e.g. Ribar, 1992), and therefore predict a large entry of women into employment (or increase in hours) when child care is subsidized. But UK work (Duncan *et al.*, 1995), using a more sophisticated model, predicts much smaller labour supply effects.

In some of these models children are treated as an outcome of economic processes. Decisions about childbearing can be analysed as a function of the time and money costs of rearing children. They are useful in explaining the way in which the national fertility rate declines as real income grows (Becker, 1989; Easterlin, 1989), and in setting up empirical hypotheses about the relationship between economic variables such as expected earnings and the childbearing decision (Ermisch, 1992).

There is also some literature, mostly empirical rather than theoretical, on 'intrahousehold' allocation (reviewed by Brannen *et al.*, 1994): How is the income coming into the household shared between household members? How is the task of managing this income shared? How is each parent's time divided between paid work, domestic work and leisure?

Children in applied economics

Applied economics describes economic conditions, usually in quantitative terms, and analyses the patterns found, using theoretical economics as a background source of hypotheses and a logical framework. It tends to describe the outcomes of economic processes, where theoretical economics tends to look at the origins. While children may not have much power as independent economic agents, they are on the receiving end of the economic decisions made by adults, and thus feature in many descriptions of economic outcomes.

A large part of this applied work is concerned with the living standards of children, with the impact on children of economic conditions, and with analysing the costs and effects of various government policies. These three types of work are considered separately below.

Children and living standards

MEASURING LIVING STANDARDS

Economics is primarily interested in people's material living standards, and how these vary within the population. Living standards depend not only on the goods and services that can be bought from disposable money income (defined usually as earnings plus social security benefits plus other income, less income tax, national insurance contributions, pensions contributions) but also on any goods and services received 'in kind' such as education and health services, together with the quality of the environment lived in.

It is rare for statistical studies, and especially those concerning children, to be able to use a measure of living standards broad enough to encompass all these features. There is a regular analysis carried out by the government statistical service of the impact of receipt of goods in kind on the distribution of income among households, but no presentation of the data in a way that shows separately the consumption by children compared to other members of the household (Office for National Statistics, 1997a). As an alternative to gross domestic product (GDP) as a measure of a nation's material standards, an index of sustainable economic welfare has been developed (Mayo, *et al.*, 1997) which allows for environmental pollution and the depletion of non-renewable resources. This shows that between 1973 and 1996 there was a 45 per cent increase in GDP per head but a 13 per cent decline in the value of the index of sustainable welfare. As yet there is no similar index at household or individual level.

Most of the work on living standards therefore examines the level and distribution of disposable money income. Income is sometimes measured both before and after housing costs as the measure of income after housing costs gives a better indication of the ability to spend from personal income. The UK government publishes an annual analysis of the distribution of income among households with below-average income (Department of Social Security, 1997) using data from the annual family expenditure survey (Office for National Statistics, 1997c). The full distribution, including households with the highest incomes, has been studied in depth by a series of analyses funded by the Joseph Rowntree Foundation (1995). This inquiry into income and wealth also examined the distribution of assets including housing, and analysed the reasons behind changes in the distribution.

Income surveys inevitably measure the income of the household rather than the individual, and so, before anything can be said about the living standards of children within the households, allowance must be made for the number of people and their ages in each household. A statistical adjustment using what are known as 'equivalence scales' is made. There are various scales, the one most frequently used is the McClements scale (McClements, 1977). Deriving a scale is a complex task. The main problem is how to separate out differences in family spending patterns that arise because some are better off than others from those that arise, regardless of living standard, because families with children spend differently from those without. Different methods can produce significantly different results and so in income distribution studies sensitivity testing is often carried out (e.g. Department of Social Security, 1997).

An alternative approach to measuring the amount of household spending devoted to children, and assessing the extent of poverty, starts by specifying a bundle of goods and services that command some kind of acceptance as a basic requirement for participation in the life of society and comparing the cost of that bundle with incomes (Family Budget Unit, 1995; Middleton *et al.*, 1997).

CHILDREN IN POVERTY

Measurements of individual income and spending are crucial in the measurement of poverty among children, and in assessing the adequacy of social security benefit levels for children and families.

As average real incomes have risen, the focus of concern about poverty has shifted to a relative rather than an absolute standard poverty. While in comparison with most children in developing countries, virtually all children in Western Europe may seem well off in absolute terms, there are many of them who are unable to participate fully in the life of the society they live in because their families have incomes far below the norm for that society. There is concern that such families' position is deteriorating (Bradshaw, 1990; Kumar, 1993; Hewlett, 1993).

One measure of poverty is the number of people living on incomes at or below income support levels, which represents a level below which the government deems people should not be allowed to fall, or income support plus a certain percentage. The most commonly used definition is half the average national income, and this is used by the European Commission as a working definition of an income below which there will be 'social exclusion'.

All measures show a significant increase in poverty in Britain in the period from 1979 and an especially sharp increase in poverty among children (Oppenheim and Harker, 1996). The number of children in families with incomes below half the national average (after housing costs) rose from 1.4 million in 1979 to 4.2 million in 1994/95 (Department of Social Security, 1997). Part of this trend is because large increases in real incomes among the already well-off have raised the average, so some people now fall within the definition of poverty even though their real incomes are unchanged. But the statistics also show that there has been an increase in the number of children living at an income below the 1994/95 real equivalent of half 1979 average income, from 1.4 million to 1.7 million. So for the worst-off groups of children real incomes are now actually lower than 18 years ago.

However, the real fall in income for the worst off is fairly small compared with the increase in the distance of this group's income from the average. The rise in poverty in Britain is derived from a large increase in income inequality: the gap between rich and poor has widened substantially.

The growth in inequality has come from a complex mix of changes that have nearly all pushed in the same direction. There has been a widening dispersion of earnings, with the well-paid seeing large increases in earnings while wages at the lower end of the distribution have stagnated or even fallen. There have been many changes in taxation and social security benefits: the reduction in direct taxation has reduced the tax paid by high-income groups, but the fall in the real value of tax thresholds has tended to raise the tax paid. Increases in indirect taxation have taken a higher proportion of the incomes of the poor than of the rich. Benefit levels have been increased in line with prices rather than average earnings so that those living on state benefits have seen a relative decline in their incomes. There have been sustained high levels of unemployment, and an increase in the number of people of working age outside the labour market, for instance lone parents and the long-term sick (Joseph Rowntree Foundation, 1995).

Particular groups of children are over-represented among those in poverty: children in lone-parent families, children in large families and children in families where there is no one in full-time work (Department of Social Security, 1997).

An international comparison of poverty in ten developed countries (Australia, Canada, France, Germany, Italy, Luxembourg, the Netherlands, Sweden, the UK and the US) using data from the mid-1980s from the Luxembourg Income Study, found that the US had by far the highest proportion of children in families below half average income (29.6 per cent) and Sweden the lowest (4.4 per cent) (Kennedy *et al.*, 1996). The UK was in the middle range (16.7 per cent), but has deteriorated since. This study was also able to measure poverty in six of these countries using a measure of income including the value of education and health services received in kind, and an imputed value of owner-occupied housing and government non-cash housing benefits. Because some of these expenditures are universal and others are concentrated on the less well-off these figures showed a much smaller proportion of children living below half average income (including the national average value of the services) and the ranking between countries little changed.

CHILDREN AND SOCIAL SECURITY BENEFITS

Studies of income and spending have been used to consider the adequacy of benefit levels. The key social security benefits for children in the UK are child benefit, and additions for children (varying by age) in the means-tested benefits.

The work on equivalence scales is especially relevant to the relative amounts that the benefits give for children in each age group, and the amounts for children relative to a couple. Income support allowances for children relative to the adult couple are actually slightly higher, especially when the family premiums in income support are included, than would be derived from the McClements scales, while both the income support allowances and the McClements scales give a figure for 11- to 15-year-olds about 50 per cent higher than for children under 11. Some more recent work (Dickens *et al.*, 1995) supports a differential of this magnitude between younger and older children, but other work finds that younger children cost the same as (Berthoud and Ford, 1996), or not much less than (Middleton *et al.*, 1997), older children. Dickens *et al.* (1995) find that the cost of a child is significantly higher in a lone-parent family compared to a couple family, and this supports the retention and possible strengthening of the single-parent premium in income support and the one-parent benefit in child benefit. The most recent (1998) government decision to cut benefits for lone parents has failed to acknowledge this evidence.

All studies of actual spending conclude that the income support allowances are inadequate for meeting a basic standard of living for a family with children. Using a budget standard for different family types, including items if more than half the population have them or they are regarded as necessities in public opinion surveys, the Family Budget Unit shows that income support for a couple with two children represents only 39 per cent of this 'modest but adequate' budget (Oppenheim and Harker, 1996). Using a specially designed national survey of children, Middleton *et al.*, (1997) show that child benefit meets approximately one-fifth of average spending on children, and that income support allowances provide between 57 per cent (children under 11 years) and 82 per cent (children aged 16 years) of what is actually being spent on children in families who are on income support. Not surprisingly they then find that many adults in these families, especially lone parents, go without basic necessities. Some studies (Berthoud and Ford, 1996; Middleton, *et al.*, 1997) conclude that the shortfall is worse for children under 11 than older children.

International studies of social security benefits (including benefits in kind) for families and children find that Britain is in the middle of the range in terms of the generosity of its benefits for children (Bradshaw, *et al.*, 1993).

Impact on children of economic circumstances

A second strand of work in applied economics looks at the impact of economic factors on outcomes for children. Bradshaw (1990) and Kumar (1993) describe the evidence for the generally adverse impact on children of living in poor economic circumstances. These effects pervade all facets of children's lives. Children from poor families are more likely to suffer ill health, accidents and premature death; they are more likely to be born with low birthweight and to attain lower heights at maturity; their educational achievement tends to be lower; they are more likely to be involved in criminal activities as teenagers and later as adults; they are more likely to suffer child abuse and being taken into care. Much of the work on the economic impact on children is done within social research that looks at economic factors as but one among the many influences on children. A major task is to unravel the interaction of the factors and to attempt to isolate the influence of each.

For instance, in attempting to unravel the reasons why the children of lone parents tend to have lower levels of educational achievement and poorer outcomes in a range of dimensions compared with children from intact families (Burghes, 1994), it is critically important for policy purposes to establish what contribution is made by each of the factors and how they interact: the disruption and distress generally accompanying the transition to lone parenthood, the difficulties a parent has in bringing up a child alone, the commonly experienced poor relationship between the lone parent and the absent parent, the frequently total loss of contact between child and absent parent, the generally low living standard of the lone-parent families (often a substantial reduction from pre-separation income and housing standard), the lack of anyone in employment. Only if the role of each can be established can policy-makers be confident that they are designing the most effective and cost-effective programmes and policies intended to help the children of lone parents to better outcomes. A long research agenda remains to give a full understanding (Burghes, 1994).

The connection between ill health and early mortality has been more thoroughly studied than some subjects. For instance, Power *et al.*, (1991) have examined a range of variables affecting the health of young adults and found that rarely is there a single dominant factor. Circumstances at birth, economic circumstances during childhood, social class of family and own education, behaviour such as smoking and drinking, all tended to play a part, but this kind of work is important in sorting out the contribution of each.

In Britain, despite continued improvements generally in health and life expectancy, there are wide social class differences in health: in 1988/89 infant mortality among babies born to fathers in unskilled manual occupations was 1.89 times that of babies born to fathers in professional occupations (Kumar, 1993). This kind of differential, in both mortality and morbidity, has been found with all sorts of measures of economic status: housing tenure, income, car ownership and unemployment. Inequalities in health have been widening.

Work by Wilkinson (1994) shows that the degree of relative poverty in a society is a significant factor in explaining health inequalities and a number of other adverse conditions for children, over and above the influence of absolute poverty. Comparisons between countries, between states in the US, and between local authority areas in Britain have all found that there is a significant association between the health and mortality of the population and the degree of income inequality within the area after taking account of variations in absolute levels of average income (Kaplan *et al.*, 1996; Kennedy *et al.*, 1996, Ben-Shlomo *et al* 1996). These findings strongly support the emphasis placed on relative poverty and prove that some of the income-related adverse outcomes can be reduced only by tackling inequality as well as the living standards of the worst off.

Some studies have been especially valuable in highlighting the adverse effect on children on some usually welcomed aspects of a modern economy. Economic progress, measured simply by rising national income, hides a deterioration in some aspects of the quality of life. Comparing English schoolchildren aged 7 to 11 in 1971 and 1990, Hillman (1993) shows that there has been a significant reduction in children's independent mobility. In 1971 three-quarters of children were allowed to cross roads on their own, but this had fallen to a half by 1990. In 1971 three-quarters owned a bicycle and two-thirds of them were allowed to cycle on the roads; in 1990 nine out of ten owned a bicycle but only one in four were allowed to cycle on the roads. Growing affluence has given priority to the needs of the increasing number of private car users, to the detriment of children's safety. And the rising incidence of asthma and other respiratory problems shows the detriment to their health.

Rosenbaum (1993) reviews the impact on children of environmental pollution and global warming. These environmental side-effects of economic development go unrecorded in gross national product except in so far as resources are used for cleaning and curing (and then these expenditures are added to GNP rather than subtracted). Children are especially vulnerable to pollution.

Policy analysis

This third category overlaps to some extent with the previous two. Both of the preceding kinds of research have policy implications. But there is another category of research that is specifically designed to evaluate options for changes in policy and practice.

Economic evaluation of policy innovations and service developments takes the form of cost-effectiveness or cost–benefit analysis (see Holtermann, 1998). These consider both the costs of alternative policies and programmes and their expected outcomes, measuring these in monetary terms where this is appropriate, and also examining distributional questions: Who gains? Who loses? Who bears the cost?

A requirement for economic evaluation is measurement of outcomes of the alternative policies or practices under consideration. When evaluations of practical effectiveness are being carried out, it is a relatively easy task to extend the analysis to encompass monetary costs and benefits. The additional requirements are a full description of the resources used in the policies and programmes, the prices of those resources, and the magnitude of any savings that can be made in other programmes.

There is a dearth of cost-effectiveness studies of social welfare programmes and policies (Holtermann, 1995; Holtermann, 1998). In part this is because few social interventions have been subjected to sufficiently rigorous evaluation of their effectiveness, using methods such as prospective randomized controlled trials or retrospective case control studies, which would enable one to conclude with some confidence that a particular policy change, or increase in spending, would bring significant benefits in relation to its cost. The few studies that can be found are often American. Symptomatic of this gap is the frequency with which the results of the High/Scope Perry Preschool programme for early education are quoted (Schweinhart *et al.*, 1993); it is not just that they are so striking, but also that there is little else with comparable rigour.

Barnardo's have published papers (Macdonald and Roberts, 1995; Alderson *et al.*, 1996; Oakley and Roberts, 1996) which describe the lack of rigorous research being carried out into the effectiveness of social welfare interventions for children. They discuss the practical feasibility and ethical aspects of randomized controlled trials, and the superiority of this research method in supporting conclusions. They give examples of good (and bad) practice.

Numerous studies describe processes and practices and are useful in their own right, but are not really evaluations. Rarely are they set up as prospective studies to examine the outcomes of alternative approaches, with inclusion of a do-nothing or do-minimum option, intervention and control groups, and a long enough follow-up period to answer the important questions.

Effectiveness studies seek to answer the question: What works? Economic evaluation addresses the further question: What works best in relation to cost? Without effectiveness studies and economic evaluation, pressure for policy change lacks the evidence-based support it needs to make it convincing.

In the field of health the position is better than in education and welfare, partly because there is a well-established role for randomized controlled trials and other techniques for comparing outcomes in assessing the effectiveness of medical interventions. The ethical issues arising from denying some people a service that might be beneficial have been well considered. Large numbers of health economists are engaged in carrying out cost-effectiveness studies of health service developments, working in partnership with medical researchers and administrators. But even here there is a shortage of sound evaluation studies. The UK Department of Health publishes a register of economic evaluations of health care treatments and programmes. In a review of the methodological quality of 200 studies, including those on the register, Mason and Drummond (1995) found that 55 were 'irretrievably flawed', that only a small minority were based directly on randomized control trial data, and that many others, of varying quality, relied on modelling techniques to quantify the impact on outcomes.

Market failure and the role of the state

Before we move on to discuss the ways in which economic policies might be most fruitfully altered for the benefit of children, it is worth making a digression on the underpinnings that theoretical economics provides for government intervention in economic affairs.

The last two decades have seen a great effort in economic policy to move the economy closer to the paradigm of the competitive market. The foundation for this is the conviction that the competitive market has desirable outcomes that cannot be achieved in other ways.

The standard microeconomics textbook devotes many chapters to analysing the working of the competitive market (e.g. Begg *et al.*, 1994). The theory has the logical structure: if A then B. There are rather a lot of clauses in A. The theory of perfectly competitive equilibrium says that if there are many suppliers of a commodity or service, acting competitively as price-takers, and prices are fully flexible up and down, if producers seek to maximize profits and consumers to maximize their own welfare subject to their budget constraints, if both producers and consumers have perfect information and there is no uncertainty, if there are no economies of scale, no external effects, and no public goods, then (and there are three main clauses in B) markets are cleared (i.e. supply equals demand in all markets), production is efficient (i.e. it is not possible to have more of one commodity without having less of another), and the allocation of resources between consumers is 'Pareto-optimal' (i.e. it is not possible to make one person better off without making someone else worse off).

The logic is flawless, but many of the clauses within A are obviously false. Many entrepreneurs and individuals have objectives much wider than just the pursuit of profit or their own welfare; lack of information about product quality or performance affects many economic choices; many markets have only a few key players and they can effectively set prices; economies of scale abound; a small number of multinationals dominate the international economy; external effects such as pollution are a major element within any economy and pollution is a form of public bad.

And if the conditions in A do not hold, then the outcomes in B may not. The failure of the conditions in A to hold, referred to as 'market failure', has been used to justify many of the government's interventions in the economy. The existence of public goods, external effects, imperfect information and monopoly power is countered by the direct provision of public goods (e.g. national defence, police, public health measures) or by regulation (e.g. health and safety regulations). The potential for abuse by monopoly suppliers can be avoided by direct provision by nationalized industries (as well as controls on monopolies and mergers), but in an alternative approach, a major element of economic policy of the past twenty years has been designed to introduce competitive structures – many suppliers and a separation of sellers and buyers – into the supply side of the economy by privatization of the nationalized industries (with regulation), and the introduction of internal markets into the public sector. The idea was that the benefits of competition could in this way be achieved without the need for government intervention.

However, as Ormerod (1994) spells out in his devastating critique of traditional economics, *The Death of Economics*, this policy of making the market more 'perfect' rather than dealing with the effects of imperfections ignores a number of fundamental results within theoretical economics itself that completely undermine the logical basis for thinking that the free market is always best.

First there is the theory of 'second best', which says in effect that there will not necessarily be a welfare gain by moving some of the economy nearer to the perfectly competitive paradigm unless all parts of it conform. For instance, the policies of privatization of public utilities and internal markets in public services give little account to the administrative cost and wastefulness of competitive activity. Competition imparts an incentive to each producer to have surplus capacity to deal with the fluctuations in demand arising from success (or failure) in attracting business from competitors; it uses resources for advertising, promotions and product differentiation to expand market share. It applies pressure to reduce cost instead of improving quality and thereby introduces incentives to suppress information about quality and performance.

Second, mathematical economists have proved that in a world with uncertainty competitive equilibrium may exist but is not necessarily a Pareto optimum. Yet few would deny that uncertainty is the norm. Third, they have shown that even a small modification to the standard assumption to allow economic agents to have at least some influence over prices leads to significantly different predictions from the model, so the outcome of policy may be quite different from what was expected. And fourth, real economies are likely to have multiple equilibrium positions, so that the outcome of policies for the free market can be a dramatic shift towards a new and unknown equilibrium rather than a move towards a near one.

The house of cards collapses. Yet the main finding of 'welfare economics' – that a perfectly competitive equilibrium is efficient and Pareto-optimal – has been persistently used to justify the shift towards competition. This is an abuse of economics for ideological purposes, and the fault lies with the politicians rather than the economists, whose exposure of the weakness of this simple proposition has been ignored.

A final, and particularly invidious, feature of the pursuit of the free market is that it virtually ignores the distributional consequences of this mode of economic management. Another large part of government activity is concerned with the distribution of income and consumption between consumers. The government shifts the allocation towards a more equal distribution through taxation and social security benefits and the provision in kind of goods such as health and education where the aim is that everyone should have an equal opportunity for services. Pareto-optimal allocations can be very unequal, and a move to the free market may increase inequality, but this possible consequence has often been treated in a cavalier way as simply a price that has to be paid for the benefits of economic efficiency and growth. Eighteen years of the pursuit of free-market economics coincided with a substantial rise in average real income per head in Britain, but an actual fall in the real incomes of people in the lowest quintile of the income distribution. Thus, the free-market economy certainly has not protected the weakest in the economy.

Between 1980/81 and 1991/92 there was a small reduction in public spending (Holtermann, 1995), and there may well be scope within the public services to reduce waste and bureaucracy and increase innovation. However, there is more expressed support for the expansion of services than for their curtailment. The British Social Attitudes Surveys (quoted by Holtermann, 1995) show that the proportion of the population expressing approval of increased taxes to pay for additional public services rose significantly during the 1980s, and the proportion saying that they thought tax levels for those with highest incomes were too low also rose.

One frequently expressed illogicality concerning the share of public services in the national economy needs to be exposed. It is often said that a service or benefit will be expanded from the gains of economic growth. This is a chimera. To achieve a real expansion of a service requires an increase in the share of that service in the national economy. The public services are very labour intensive. For instance, over 80 per cent of schools' budgets are directly accounted for by staff, and a proportion of the rest will also be labour costs. If national income grows, income per head and average earnings will normally also grow. If teachers and other staff involved in education are to share in any growth in the economy, their wages must rise in line with average earnings. So, the share of education in the national economy will be exactly the same as before, and there will be no increase in the amount of educational services provided, even though there will be an increase in 'real' (i.e. after adjusting for price inflation) spending on education. Unless educational staff are to be denied the increase in earnings enjoyed by the working population as a whole, then an increase in educational services will occur only if its share of national income increases. In fact, spending on education is expected to be 4.9 per cent of GDP in 1996/97 compared to 5.4 per cent in 1978/79 (HM Treasury, 1997).

Policies for children and the future

The relevance to children of this digression on 'welfare economics' is that they are the ones who will have to live with the long-term consequences of today's decisions about economic management. And it is not obvious that the long-term effects are being given any kind of systematic consideration in the formation of economic policy, which tends to have a short time horizon.

A review carried out for Barnardo's of the impact of public expenditure and fiscal policies on Britain's children and young people (Holtermann, 1995) suggested a number of key areas of economic policy where reform would lead to a better present and future life for children:

1. *Employment*. In pursuit of economic growth and the control of inflation, macroeconomic policies have allowed persistently high un-employment. Microeconomic policies to foster flexibility in the labour market through curbs on trade union power and deregulation have allowed low wages to fall even further in relation to the average and labour market insecurity to grow.

2. *The growth of poverty and inequality*. First and foremost, living in poverty is miserable and leads to all kinds of adverse outcomes for the people concerned, and this on its own is enough to justify moves to reduce it. But second, it actually places a burden on the rest of society (Holtermann, 1996; Glyn and Miliband, 1994). Poverty has distributional implications: the rest of society pays for supporting the living standards of low-income people through social security benefits. If sufficient public spending were devoted to curing poverty – through job creation for the unemployed and child care services for all parents who wish to work, together with a rise in social security benefits for those who cannot work to a level that gave all citizens the ability to participate fully – the charge on the well-off section of the community would be much greater than it is now. In addition, the existence of poverty has adverse effects on economic efficiency: resources are used on providing additional health and educational facilities, social services and the criminal justice system, to deal with misfortunes that are more common among the poor. Some of this expenditure could be avoided or diverted to improving universal services if poverty and inequality were reduced.

3. *Underfunding of public services*. A long list can be drawn up where there would appear to be a strong case for expecting further investment in children to provide benefits in relation to its cost (Holtermann, 1995). (Though as I said earlier, the sound research to back this up is often lacking.) Even where initiatives are made they tend to be limited through

means-testing or targeting at deprived areas or restricted to children in need, and are often funded at a level that permits dealing with evident problems with little left for preventive work. While means-testing may keep spending down, it has the effect of trapping people in low incomes – as earnings rise, benefits or services are withdrawn at such a rate that people are hardly any better off. It also has the effect of entrenching even further the divide between people in our society with enough income to live independently of means-tested help and those below this line.

4. *Environmental decline*. Some steps in the right direction have been taken: a landfill tax has been introduced, progressive increases in petrol duties are being maintained. But in many instances action has not matched rhetoric, and many opportunities have been passed by: the rate of VAT on all home insulation could be reduced to 8 per cent to match the VAT rate on domestic fuel; a higher proportion of farming subsidies could be tied to using farming methods that do not damage wildlife; recycling targets could be increased and backed by greater efforts to see them achieved; greater support at the international level to help developing countries to shift to less polluting industrial processes could be given, and so on. The actions taken so far are not enough to halt environmental decline.

In all these areas, a redirection of policy could achieve significant and lasting benefit. There might be some consequential reduction in economic growth, but given the environmental damage being done by our ever-increasing consumption, and the fact that the fruits of economic growth are not filtering down to the worst off, one has to question how much this matters.

Conclusion

Children are rarely the centre of attention in theoretical economics, which concentrates on how adults wield their economic power. Children are largely treated in economic theory as but one of many influences on adults' decisions. In contrast, there is a considerable amount of work in applied economics with children as the focal point. This shows that they are disproportionately represented among the poorest in society and that the levels of social security benefits are insufficient for full participation in mainstream life. To take a long-term view, a number of current economic policies would appear to be ill designed for achieving the well-being of future generations, especially in the fields of employment, poverty and the environment. At some time in the future, today's children may look back in anger at some of the economic decisions being made today on their behalf.

References

Alderson, P. *et al.* (1996) *What Works? Effective Social Interventions in Child Welfare.* Barkingside: Barnardo's.

Becker, G. (1965) A theory of the allocation of time. *Economic Journal*, 75, (September), 493–517.

Becker, G. (1989) Family. In J. Eatwell, M. Milgate and P. Newman (eds), *The New Palgrave: Social Economics.* London: Macmillan.

Begg, D., Fischer, S. and Dornbusch, R. (1994) *Economics*, 4th edition. London: McGraw Hill.

Ben-Shlomo, Y., White, I. and Marmot, M. (1996) Does the variation in the socioeconomic characteristics of an area affect mortality? *British Medical Journal*, 312 (20 April), 1013–14.

Berthoud, R. and Ford, R. (1996) A new way of measuring relative financial needs. Joseph Rowntree Foundation Social Policy Research Findings 109.

Bradshaw, J. (1990) *Child Poverty and Deprivation in the UK.* National Children's Bureau.

Bradshaw, J., Ditch, J., Holmes, H. and Whiteford, P. (1993) Support for Children: a comparison of arrangements in fifteen countries. Department of Social Security Research Report no. 21. London: HMSO.

Brannen, J., Meszaros, G., Moss, P. and Poland, G. (1994) Employment and family life: a review of research in the UK (1980–1994). Employment Department Research Series no. 41. Sheffield: Department of Employment.

Browning, M. (1992) Children and household economic behaviour. *Journal of Economic Literature*, 30, 1434–75.

Burghes, L. (1994) *Lone Parenthood and Family Disruption: The Outcomes for Children.* London: Family Policy Studies Centre.

Department of Social Security (1997) *Households below Average Income: A Statistical Analysis 1979–1994/95.* London: The Stationery Office.

Dickens, R., Fry, V. and Pashardes, P. (1995) The cost of children and the welfare state. Joseph Rowntree Foundation Social Policy Research Findings 89.

Duncan, A., Giles, C. and Webb, S. (1995) *The Impact of Subsidising Childcare.* Manchester: Equal Opportunities Commission.

Easterlin, R. (1989) Fertility. In J. Eatwell, M. Milgate and P. Newman, (eds), *The New Palgrave: Social Economics.* London: Macmillan.

Ermisch, J. (1992) *Lone Parenthood: An Economic Analysis.* Cambridge: Cambridge University Press.

Family Budget Unit (1995) *Modest but Adequate: Summary Budgets for Sixteen Households.* Family Budget Unit.

Glyn, A. and Miliband, D. (eds) (1994) *Paying for Inequality: The Economic Cost of Social Injustice.* London: Institute of Public Policy Research.

Hewlett, S. (1993) *Child Neglect in Rich Nations*. New York: United Nations Children's Fund.

Hillman, M. (ed.) (1993) *Children, Transport and the Quality of Life*. London: Policy Studies Institute.

HM Treasury (1997) Public expenditure: statistical analyses 1997–98. Cm 3601.

Holtermann, S. (1995) *All Our Futures: The Impact of Public Expenditure and Fiscal Policies on Britain's Children and Young People*. Barkingside: Barnardo's.

Holtermann, S. (1996) The cost of poverty: a report for Fulcrum Productions. Available at http://www.channel4.com.

Holtermann, S. (1998) *Weighing It Up: The Application of Economic Evaluations to Social Welfare Programmes*. York: Joseph Rowntree Foundation.

Joseph Rowntree Foundation (1995) *Inquiry into Income and Wealth*, Vols 1 and 2.

Kaplan, G. *et al.* (1996) Inequality in income and mortality in the United States: analysis of mortality and potential pathways. *British Medical Journal*, **312** (20 April), 999–1003.

Kennedy, B. *et al.* (1996) Income distribution and mortality: cross sectional ecological study of the Robin Hood index in the United States. *British Medical Journal*, **312** (20 April), 1004–07.

Kennedy, S., Whiteford, P. and Bradshaw, J. (1996) The economic circumstances of children in ten countries. In J. Brannen and M. O'Brien (eds), *Children in Families: Research and Policy*. London: Falmer Press.

Kumar, V. (1993) *Poverty and Inequality in the UK: The Effects on Children*. National Children's Bureau.

Lister, R. (1992) *Women's Economic Dependency and Social Security*. Manchester: Equal Opportunities Commission.

McClements, L. (1977) Equivalence scales for children. *Journal of Public Economics*, **8** (2), 191–210.

Macdonald, G. and Roberts, H. (1995) *What Works in the Early Years? Effective Interventions for Children and Their Families in Health, Social Welfare, Education and Child Protection*. Barkingside: Barnardo's.

Mason, J. and Drummond, M. (1995) The DH register of cost-effectiveness studies: a review of study content and quality. Centre for Health Economics Discussion Paper 128, York.

Mayo, E., MacGillivray, A. and McLaren, D. (1997) More isn't always better: a special briefing on growth and quality of life in the UK. London: New Economics Foundation and Friends of the Earth.

Middleton, S., Ashworth, K. and Braithwaite, I. (1997) Expenditure on children in Great Britain. Joseph Rowntree Foundation, Social Policy

Research Findings 118.

Oakley, A. and Roberts, H. (eds) (1996) *Evaluating Social Interventions*. Barkingside: Barnardo's.

Office for National Statistics (1997a) The effects of taxes and benefits on household income 1995–1996. *Economic Trends*, March.

Office for National Statistics (1997b) *Children's Spending*. London: HMSO.

Office for National Statistics (1997c) *Family Spending 1995–96*. London: HMSO.

Oppenheim, C. and Harker, L. (1996) *Poverty: The Facts*, 3rd edition. Child Poverty Action Group.

Ormerod, P. (1994) *The Death of Economics*. London: Faber and Faber.

Power, C., Manor, O. and Fox, J. (1991) *Health and Class: The Early Years*. London: Chapman and Hall.

Ribar, D. (1992) Child care and the labour supply of married women. *Journal of Human Resources*, **27** (1), 135–65.

Rosenbaum, M. (1993) *Children and the Environment*. National Children's Bureau.

Schweinhart, L., Barnes, H. and Weikart, D. (1993) *Significant Benefits: The High/Scope Perry Preschool Study through age 27*. Ypsilant: High/Scope Press.

Wilkinson, R. (1994) *Unfair Shares: The Effects of Widening Income Differences on the Welfare of the Young*. Barkingside: Barnardo's.

4

Children and Europe

Crescy Cannan

Introduction

'Children and Europe' is a wide topic. Not only are there varying attitudes
to children and childhood in Europe, but there are very different
approaches to services for children and families. Then there are
contemporary issues concerning children – such as the impact of racism
on minorities, violence, and the sexual victimization of children in the
family and in the public sphere. Of growing concern worldwide are the
consequences for children growing up in armed conflict, with the
associated difficulties of refugees and asylum seekers. For the purposes
of the chapter I will focus on family policy within the European Union
(EU) states, considering the field from the perspective of children, bearing
in mind the shift of principle (if not always of practice) introduced by the
1989 UN Convention on the Rights of the Child. The meaning of
children's rights – and welfare – is still contested, as I shall show in
unravelling aspects of family policy. By children I usually mean children
and young people up to the age of 18, though the trend to extend
dependence on parents into young people's twenties can make such a cut-
off point problematic.

Therborn (1996) argues that we are in a new, internationalized stage of
child politics. The first was that from the end of the nineteenth century to
the creation of the post-Second World War welfare states in which
children saw some paternalistic protection from the harshness of
employment and over-zealous parental power through schooling and
welfare systems. In contrast, in the contemporary stage, the UN
Convention brings a notion of human rights into the world of children
and does so with *all* children in mind, not just the 'exceptions' with
problems. While the inter-war movements for child welfare were certainly
international (exemplified in the Save the Children Fund working for
victims of the First World War), the contemporary stage is characterized
by very active non-governmental organizations (NGOs) mediating

between governments, local welfare systems and supranational bodies: the United Nations, the Council of Europe (with its Commission on Human Rights) and the European Union. There are differences in countries' responses to the convention. Traditionally Catholic countries and welfare organizations have tended to interpret the convention as meaning measures to strengthen the family, whereas social democratic countries and Scandinavian and left-oriented organizations have stressed children's independent interests. I shall explore some of these differences, turning first to the social context of childhood in the European Union.

Demographic changes in the European family

During the twentieth century the child population has fallen from one-third to one-fifth, as a proportion of the population of the EU (European Commission 1994, p. 98). There are paradoxes. Qvortrup (1995) notes that while European adults seem to like children, to want children and to say they should be given first priority, in fact they are having fewer of them, children's lives are becoming more and more organized, and parents are spending less time with them. This is especially true of fathers, whose time at work has increased over recent years and who are still reluctant to take paternity and parental leave (European Commission, 1994, pp. 113–19; Hobcraft and Kiernan, 1995, p. 38)

Demographic data on EU member states are available from Eurostat, which works to the European Commission; and, in relation to families, from the European Observatory on National Family Policies established in 1989 (reported by Ditch *et al.*, 1996a, b). By 1993 all EU countries' fertility levels were well below the replacement level of 2.1 children per woman. This is because women are postponing childbearing until they are in their thirties, although Britain is notable for its high rate of teenage pregnancies, which at 3 per cent of 15- to 19-year-olds giving birth is three times as high as the rate in the Netherlands and France.

There are different reasons in different countries for the falling birth rate: Germany has a high proportion of childless women; France has fewer childless women than it did earlier this century, but family size has fallen dramatically (Hantrais, 1996, p. 58). Northern countries' rates began declining first in the late 1960s, followed a decade later by a rapid fall in rates in the southern countries and Ireland. Spain and Italy now have the lowest fertility levels in the industrialized world (Ditch *et al.*, 1996a, p. 28). In Germany, including the eastern Länder, this has meant that the numbers of children and young people under 18 fell from 21.3 million in 1971 to 15.5 million in 1991 while the over-60s rose from 15 to 16.4 million. However, while pensions have been protected, the real value of child benefits after the first child (including tax allowances) has been eroded (Lawson, 1996, pp. 38–44). On the other hand, Ireland decided to increase child benefits once the decline in births was obvious (Ditch *et al.*, 1996a, p. 29).

The implications of this demographic change for children have hardly been considered in policy terms in Britain, but this increase in child solitude and segregation from the wider society (Qvortrup, 1995; Moss and Petrie, 1997) has received public attention in Germany, where some 50 per cent of children are only children (Lawson, 1996, p. 40). Here pre-school provision and family or mothers' centres are designed to provide informal social experiences for children as well as for parents, part of striving to create a child-friendly public life and to raise awareness of the need for better urban design, traffic management and a healthier environment (Gerzer-Sass and Pettinger, 1996).

These dramatic changes in birth rates are not fully understood, but they may be associated with the opportunity costs of having a child. This cost is higher in southern countries, where there is relatively little in the social package (benefits and services) offered parents. Hobcraft and Kiernan (1995, pp. 46–51) observe that the contrast in fertility rates is most extreme between southern Europe and Scandinavia with France, Germany, the Netherlands and the UK falling in between. While all north-western countries have a higher level of welfare support and acknowledge a wider variety of family forms than do the southern countries, it is the Scandinavian countries which also promote gender equity and a greater emphasis on practical support for parenthood and for women, thus sharing the burden to a greater degree and so perhaps marginally adding to the higher fertility levels of those countries. It is interesting that the long-term natalist policies in France do not seem to have increased the birth rate (which is slightly lower than that of the UK), though the associated support for parents may encourage women to have children earlier (Ditch *et al.*, 1996a, p. 29). I will look at the child support package later (p. 59), but first I turn to the changing family forms within which children live.

Everyone knows that family forms have everywhere become more 'diverse, complex and volatile' (Ditch *et al.*, 1996a, p. 30). Again the northern countries are leading, but the same trends are appearing in the south. The number of marriages has declined in all countries and marriage is occurring later, usually after a period of cohabitation. Remarriage had increased but is now in decline, although remarriages made up more than a quarter of all marriages in 1993 in Denmark and the UK, the countries with the highest EU levels of marriage breakdown. Everywhere there is an increase of births outside marriage – about 30 per cent in the UK by 1993 and about 50 per cent in Denmark. Cohabitation is long established in Scandinavia and has rapidly emerged also in Belgium, the UK, France, Luxembourg, the Netherlands and Germany. Ireland and the southern countries still have very low levels. A high proportion of births outside marriage are assumed to be to children within cohabitations (Ditch *et al.*, 1996a, pp. 32–3). In France, 30 per cent of children were born out of wedlock in 1990, but 60 per cent of these children were recognized at birth by their fathers (Hantrais, 1996, p. 58).

All EU countries have seen an increase in lone parenthood, ranging from 20 per cent of families in Denmark, 19 per cent in the UK, 15 per cent in Germany, 10 per cent in France to 5.6 per cent in Greece (Ditch *et al.*, 1996a, pp. 34–5). By the early 1990s one French child in four was living with stepbrothers and sisters (Hantrais, 1996, p. 59). The greater proportion of lone parents in France is a result of divorce or separation; it is the UK which has the highest proportion of single or never married lone parents, the group most at risk of poverty (Ditch *et al.*, 1996a, pp. 34–5).

Family policy and the EU

The treaties which created the European Union, culminating in the 1992 Maastricht Treaty, do not deal with families or children in any explicit or direct sense. Such social policy as exists is to do with the social protection, and employment and training rights of workers, with the underlying aim of promoting competition, growth and mobility of labour. In accordance with principles of subsidiarity, family policies and social services are taken to be matters for national governments rather than the EU. However, the divide is not clear-cut in practice; in the areas of promoting equal opportunities between men and women the European Commission has for more than 20 years promoted policies which have benefited women and their children (Hantrais, 1995). Often through the Social Fund, the UK has seen many projects which bring women into education, training and employment opportunities, and which include day care for children. The programmes, however, are aimed at the needs of the parents (workers) rather than those of the children.

The Commission and its Employment and Social Affairs Directorate (known as DG-V), however, are increasingly finding that matters concerning families and children are coming their way. Social action programmes have encouraged the sharing of experience in order to disseminate innovative and effective new practices in training and local social development. These emphasize participartory approaches, which is usually taken to mean a key role for NGOs, including both established voluntary-sector organizations and local community groups. These NGO networks have been important, not just in disseminating new ideas, but in lobbying at the EU level as well as within member states. In the children and families field there is the Confederation of Family Organisations in Europe (COFACE) and the European Forum for Child Welfare (EFCW).

Furthermore, the UN Convention on the Rights of the Child has raised the profile of children, and the EFCW (the European branch of the International Federation for Child Welfare) was formed in 1991 with a membership of 20 countries. The EFCW is committed to full implementation of the UN Convention and, like the Council of Europe (based in Strasbourg, with a membership of 25 countries) and the European Parliament, regards the matter as one now on the public agenda. Children are viewed not only as the objects of policy or an adjunct of labour market needs but as requiring coherent and integrated services. To this end the EFCW calls for an EU Charter on the rights of the child and incorporation of the needs of children in EU legislation, directives, policies and programmes.

The European Commission presented the Council of Ministers with a communication on family policy in 1989. As a result it was decided that more information was needed on demographic patterns and family policies in member states (hence the setting up of the Observatory), and that the impact of the policies of the then European Community on the family needed more consideration. The Commission went further, issuing a statement in the same year on the need to promote policies which recognized the principle of reconciling family and work life. Underlining the strong emphasis in EU policy on solidarity, the Commission stated that

> the family assumes an essential role and place in the cohesion and future of society. Therefore it should be protected and specific measures adopted in recognition of the services it renders society ... the appropriateness of Community interest is based less on ideological grounds but more on such objective facts as the economic role of the family, the importance of the family as a touchstone for solidarity between generations, the irreversible desire for equality between men and women and the wish of women to have complete access to working life. (Communication COM (89)363, quoted in Ditch *et al.*, 1996a, pp. 7–8).

The family dimension within the Commission of the EU was strengthened by calls in 1991 from the European Parliament for publicly funded, widely available and good-quality child care services for children up to the age of 10. Then in 1992 the Council of Ministers issued a Recommendation on Childcare which acknowledged that if family and work obligations are to be reconciled, there is a need for affordable, accessible, diverse, flexible and multifunctional child care services. In 1994, during the International Year of the Family, the European Parliament called for a stronger commitment to tackling social exclusion and bringing about equal opportunities for women by stronger policies on parental leave, part-time work, child care services, social protection and continuing education and training, together with more research on the changing nature of families (Ditch *et al.*, 1996a, p. 9). Partly owing to British blocking, such policies have been weaker than they might have been, but the issue of family life is at least on the official agenda. It remains, however, as Bronwen Cohen of Children in Scotland and Vice-President of COFACE says, 'unsatisfactory that the European childcare policies consider the role of child care in facilitating access to the labour market but not in meeting children's needs' (Cohen, 1995, p. 41).

The European Commission Network on Child Care, in its work within equal opportunity programmes from 1986 to 1996, has shown how this might be achieved. The Network has collected information and disseminated examples of good practice (some of which are referred to below) with the intention of promoting clearer criteria for quality in services for young children. It echoes the EFCW 1995 position statement on principles and quality in services for young children and the Council of Europe 1996 strategy for children, and has established quality targets for child care which, it argues, are attainable by the year 2006. It calls for services which recognize lifestyle and ethnic diversity, and insists that the old narrow European Community focus on child care as merely provision for working parents is an inadequate response to the complex and changing society we live in. More imaginative and broader services are needed with children's well-being at their heart (European Commission Network on Childcare, 1996a, b).

However, it is hardly surprising that, as Hantrais (1995, p. 79) notes, the Commission has been reluctant to intervene in family affairs. There is considerable variation between member states in the goals and substance of family policy and child support. In the dominant states of the EU, employment records form the basis of social protection, with family affairs treated as a separate, private though fundamental domain, and at best as women's issues. On the other hand, the Scandinavian, social democratic, model is one that does give child support a high priority, as a strategy both for gender equity and to meet children's independent needs. Here entitlements are individual, rather than based on employment or dependence on a breadwinner and thus on family obligations as in the Bismarckian model (Millar and Warman, 1996). We now turn to look at these similarities and differences in family and child support within the countries of the EU.

European cash-based child support policies

'Child support' has come to mean both that money which absent parents may be required to pay for their child(ren) *and* the general package which societies have constructed to compensate parents for the costs of bearing and rearing children and to avoid the life-cycle poverty which parenting may bring. Following Bradshaw *et al.* (1993a, b) I will use the term child support to describe the package of public policies intended to benefit families. It thus includes social security benefits including child benefit, specific benefits for lone parents, children with special needs, and means-tested social assistance benefits which may or may not be used to supplement low wages. These family cash transfer payments are complemented by tax allowances, and by wider benefits such as those for housing, day care, health care and public transport. Looking simply at the level of child benefit (family allowances) will tell us little about the level of child support in a particular country because the package will vary according to these other potential or actual sources of income including wage levels. The package might also be said to include benefits in kind – education, day care, after-school care, youth clubs, health care, community family support services, and of course measures to promote women's equality and welfare. These service-based areas will be the topic of a later section (pp. 62–4).

The work of Bradshaw and Ditch for the European Observatory on National Family Policies has demonstrated how difficult it is to answer the question so often put: Which country in Europe is 'best' for children? The stereotype of high child benefits and extensive pre-school provision in France has some truth for early years and for second and subsequent children. Provision, then, may be good at certain stages and for certain groups but not necessarily across the board. Germany (like France) is well known for its strong commitment to education, training and youth services, but its pre-school provision is not very high in league tables.

Traditionally the UK has been stronger on cash benefits aimed at the very poor than continental welfare states, which protect status but do not aim to redistribute income. This means that up to the end of the 1980s we see relatively high family transfers in the UK, exceeded in the EU only by Denmark, France, Luxembourg and the Netherlands (Bradshaw *et al.*, 1993a). However, these countries have higher general social protection than the UK as well as higher levels of earnings, and the high spending in the UK may reflect greater inequalities and need rather than the achievement of higher family incomes (*ibid.*):

> Child-related spending, broadly defined, is probably highest in Belgium, Denmark and Luxembourg. France and Germany appear to fall in the next group, followed by another broad grouping of the United Kingdom, Norway and the Netherlands. Greece and Spain appear to be in the lowest grouping with Portugal and Ireland being a rank above, despite the fact that Spain has a higher income level. (*ibid.*, p. 22).

(The study also notes that provision in the US is lower than for any of these countries.) These calculations are averages. What do they mean for families in different circumstances?

On average earnings, Belgium, Luxembourg and Norway provide the most generous package to a couple with two primary school children. The range included in the child support package went from £4 in Spain to £154 in Belgium, the UK coming midway in the league table, with the Netherlands above Denmark but below Germany. (*ibid.*, p. 59)

Lone-parent families on average earnings received less than a couple family in Belgium, Germany, Greece, Italy and Portugal, whereas Norway, France and Denmark (for larger families) are all outstandingly more generous in their treatment of lone parents (*ibid.*, p. 68). 'At half average earnings, a lone parent with one child is most generously treated in Ireland and Germany and least generously treated in Portugal and Spain ... where (like Greece and Italy) little help is available to lone parents' (Ruxton, 1996, p. 109). The UK has the highest proportion of lone parents receiving means-tested benefits (84%) in contrast to the 25% of lone parents in France who do so and the 16% in Germany (Evans, 1996, pp. 45–6). As these are typically the least generous payments and are based on high levels of need, they indicate greater poverty among lone parents in the UK as well as more isolation from employment. Housing costs exert an important influence – for instance the French family becomes relatively better off after housing benefits than the family in Denmark, Netherlands and the UK. So Britain and Ireland are relatively generous in targeted benefits for low-income families but much of this is lost in higher child care and housing costs.

For families with incomes below the average, Germany, Ireland, Italy and the UK target their child benefits on lower-income families, reducing support as earnings rise, while Belgium, France, Portugal, and Luxembourg *increase* the level of support with income, partly through generous tax allowances. Denmark, the Netherlands and Norway vary it little with income (Bradshaw *et al.*, 1993a, p. 59). In France, low earners may be well supported by a high social wage or benefit package, and in contrast in Greece and Portugal low earners must usually turn to the extended family for support.

Evans' example of a model low-earning couple with two young children showed that

tax thresholds are much lower in Britain. The family would start to pay tax at 27 hours work, whereas in France it would be 41 hours and in Germany 37... In Britain, liability for tax is below income support levels for this family, whereas in France it is almost twice (195%) and in Germany 143% of social minima levels (Evans, 1996, p. 32).

This means that incentives to work are greater in France and Germany. Families in Britain are caught in a poverty trap which the current Labour government is committed to removing. Overall, then, we can see that rankings vary by family type and income level. However, Bradshaw *et al.* do conclude that:

> For lone parents who are earning Norway, France and Luxembourg are the most generous countries... The UK [is] relatively more generous to the lone parent family on benefit... For couples, Belgium, Norway, Luxembourg and France are the leaders though again Germany ... and the UK do better for the lowest paid and Denmark does better for the worst case [of the lone-parent family on benefit] (Bradshaw *et al.*, 1993a, p. 70).

Early-years services

The provision of services for young children has been affected by two developments since the late 1980s, each of which has raised the level of discussion in the EU on the provision of services for young children. First, the reunification of Germany brought into the EU an area with a high level of publicly funded provision (and despite the problems of that region, provision remains strong). Second, the accession in 1995 of Finland and Sweden to the EU brought powerful new members with highly developed services for children (Ruxton, 1996, pp. 151–2; Cohen and Hagen, 1997).

It will be interesting to see whether patterns of demand change with the trend of women taking parental leave for up to three years. Parental leave, for which there is no provision in Ireland, Luxembourg and the UK, is leave taken after maternity leave. Only the three Scandinavian countries offer substantial payment, Sweden and Finland giving the right to follow it with part-time work and a corresponding allowance. Belgium and Denmark have schemes where career breaks and leave can be taken at varied times, and nine countries offer parental leave when children are ill (Ruxton, 1996, pp. 134–45). In the case of Germany, for instance, there is a two-year child-raising allowance and three years' leave entitlement available to either parent (in practice taken by mothers) with pension credits (European Commission (DG-V) 1994, pp. 57–8). While there may be an implicit agenda here of returning women to the home, at present the equal opportunities framework of EU law means that it is operating to keep women in the labour force. In terms of child care provision, it may mean greater demand for flexible and open care facilities for infants and young children, and for more structured services between the ages of 3 and 10.

Access to services up to 3 years of age is greatest in Denmark, former

East Germany, Belgium, Sweden, France and Finland. For 3 to 6 years it is greatest in former East Germany, Belgium, France and Italy (Ruxton, 1996, p. 155, drawing on material from the EC Childcare Network). While much of recent child care development is occurring within the EU principle of reconciling work and family responsibilities (and of trying to create family-friendly workplaces), the traditional goals of early-years provision vary with welfare state models. There is a stronger emphasis on the needs of children and women in Sweden and Denmark, with France stressing these as well as the goal of family support (Ruxton, 1996, p. 96). The French state combines a traditional Catholic emphasis on the family with a strong Republican commitment to the notions of citizenship and equality of opportunity. Together with a strong position on women's opportunities since the Socialist Party's dominance during the 1980s, the result is a society which actively values day care and nursery education from the age of 2 and often younger. France sees these as important in promoting children's citizenship as well as in supporting families and working mothers, the majority of whom are in full-time jobs. Nursery schools are free; nursery care is heavily subsidized with charges in the range of 10-15 per cent of family income. Local communities have drop-in centres where parents can leave their children for a number of sessions per week. Parental participation is newish in pre-school services, and even newer (and contentious) in schools, but both are being encouraged as part of widespread measures in place for combating social exclusion and promoting 'insertion' or integration of those marginalized by poverty, poorly designed social housing schemes or racism, or by living in areas of high unemployment (Cannan, 1996).

The French system, then, offers a good range of services for children and is a highly professionalized system. Services *for* children may be an appropriate term here – the high-quality provision is not always as flexible or democratic as that in Germany, the Netherlands and Denmark. In these countries there has long been a tradition of emphasizing the social and developmental benefits for children of pre-school and educational services, alongside a radical alternative strand. While the parent-run *crèches parentales* are growing in France (subsidized by the state, with 35 per cent of the costs coming from parents), Germany has longer-established examples of self-help initiatives which strive to meet both parents' and children's needs (Gerzer-Sass and Pettinger, 1996). Some of these stress the need to avoid the over-structuring of the child's day, and to replicate as far as possible in the day care setting the spontaneous activities which would occur in the home environment. In its examples of good practice, the EC Network describes some of the care and imagination given to the design of buildings for pre-school children, and in the case of Denmark it describes a system which gives a lot of autonomy to local social affairs departments and produces a high-quality mix of public and independent centres. The flexibility of the service means a local range including, for instance, the 120 woodland kindergartens to which city children are taken daily by bus for an outdoor existence. Parents are involved in services both in daily discussions and through committees (European Commission Childcare Network, 1996b). As in Germany, there is a stress on informality, relaxation and spontaneity with sibling-like age-integrated groups. In northern Italy too there is a good deal of attention given to parental involvement, in order to support families and to prevent isolation in mothers and children in small families, and also to make nurseries enlarge their functions to become community centres and, as in France and in the best-practice family centres in the UK, contribute both to family life and to local social development (Cannan, 1996; see Ruxton, 1996, and Kamerman and Kahn, 1995, for more details and examples).

Overall, then, the EU has seen an increase in early services in most EU countries as compared with the late 1980s. Most governments have committed themselves to this expansion, together with improved parental leave entitlements. There is a search for greater diversity and flexibility in provision, so that the social goals of preventing isolation of children and of providing a safe and imaginative environment to supplement family life can be combined with good-quality care and early education. There is generally improved training for centre workers, more parental involvement, and an attempt to break down the education–care barriers in a more flexible way. However, the costs of services in most EU countries and (restrictions on public expenditure) mean that the degree of subsidy to parents seen in many EU countries may be threatened.

Child protection and youth justice

Irrespective of governments' politics, there has been a convergence in social provision for families and their children when there are difficulties. Most north-western European countries have recent legislation echoing the UN Convention on the Rights of the Child – promoting the child's right to family life and to remain with his or her family where possible, the right to protection from abuse, and the right to voice an opinion over his or her circumstances and plans. Such legislation was passed in 1982 in Sweden, 1984 in France, 1989 in England and Wales, and in 1990 in Germany (Colla-Müller, 1993; Madge, 1994; Lorenz, 1991). There is a philosophy within social services of partnership between state and parents in helping parents meet their obligations, and enabling them as far as possible to retain those responsibilities.

In parallel, a consensus has grown that smaller-scale and more open units are more helpful, whether for children, elderly people or people with disabilities or mental health problems (Colton and Hellinckx, 1994).

Across north-western Europe there has been a fall in the numbers of children and young people in residential care, with, for instance, a reduction of about one-third in France and Belgium since 1979 (Madge, 1994, pp. 50–1), and increasing use of foster care. Children's homes have become more diverse, flexible settings, partly to contain costs, but also as new settings for family support, in which families can be involved, retaining ties with children rather than losing them to the care system. Many combine day and residential provision, offering different kinds of specialist provision and acting as resource centres for families in need and for local child minders and foster parents. Residents no longer spend all aspects of their lives in the total institution but normalize their lives, attending community schools, leisure centres and health services. So the boundaries have become more flexible between residential and day institutions, between being in public care and being the responsibility of parents, or, for older children and young people, being cared for and being independent (as for instance in the successful French foyer model currently growing in the UK, and the supported housing schemes for young people in Germany). There is a recognition that services should be designed to help parents to look after children adequately, that many kinds of families will need help at some time, and that children and family and centres should measure their success in increased community use.

However, there are differences between welfare states, as we have already seen. In the case of child protection and juvenile justice, the adversarial and the inquisitorial legislative models produce very different practices. The relative merits of these two are not clear-cut and, in the case of French child protection, are still being debated by British observers. Cooper and Hetherington (1995) express admiration for the inquisitorial French children's judge and his or her discretion and power over the conduct of the case and the professionals involved, and for the flexibility in and accessibility of the system. Luckock *et al.* (1996) are more critical. They argue that the French system is based on the paternalistic authority of the judge, obscuring the conflicting interests at stake in most family disputes and privileging the family and its preservation over the rights of various parties and especially of the child. While Cooper and Hetherington argue that the French system is founded on and promotes consensus as a basis of working and thus gives a clearer mandate and sense of confidence for social workers, Luckock *et al.* are concerned that there is an assumption of parents' and social workers' agreement with judges, or at least of compliance with the judges' view. It is a system which gives little place to independent representation of the child, and here it is consistent with the Bismarckian/Napoleonic and Catholic models of social policy, which stress a strong state and family obligations. One consequence is a higher rate of children in public care than is found in the UK. In contrast, social democratic Scandinavian welfare systems tend to stress the rights of the child more than the authority of the family in their handling of child abuse and delinquency.

Definitions of child abuse vary, as do responses. Most north European states have more highly developed response systems than southern European states. Central registers are kept in Belgium, the Netherlands, Sweden and the UK, but not in Austria, France, Germany, Finland, Greece, Ireland, Italy and Spain. There is mandatory reporting in Denmark, Finland, France, Italy, Luxembourg, Portugal and Sweden (Ruxton, 1996, p. 405). There may be particular obligations of various professions. However, there is rising concern that reporting and disclosures of abuse and of sexual abuse are increasing, and there is a consensus that more research is needed, encompassing wider areas of child victimization such as prostitution, pornography, paedophilia and drug abuse. Voluntary organizations, public campaigns and helplines in these areas have increased awareness and emerged as strong agenda-setters linked internationally through the EFCW.

In the area of youth justice, common trends include more preventive schemes such as summer projects in France, and the wide range of community schemes which have tended to replace custody in the case of younger 'offenders'. While Ruxton (1996, p. 307) is concerned that there may be some degree of backlash in England, France and Denmark against these schemes, he notes that the 1980s saw a widespread swing to just these approaches, along with a tendency for the age of responsibility and of custody to rise. The populist demand for more punitive approaches might be associated with high levels of youth unemployment in France, a country whose policies have hitherto viewed youth crime as a symptom of social exclusion (Cannan, 1996). To date, this has been responded to as a question of urban regeneration, of finding constructive ways of involving young people in their cities and neighbourhoods and of getting employers to take on unemployed young people. However, some of the backlash may result from the extreme right-wing movement, which views the problems of the cities as caused by the north African population. The rise of racist organizations among young people is a matter of concern as much as the targeting of ethnic minorities in right-wing political campaigns.

Figures on the prevalence of juvenile crime are notoriously difficult to compare. The International Self-Report Delinquency Study based in Amsterdam suggests surprisingly that England and Wales have a much lower than average delinquency rate, but there appears to be great similarity in the nature of the offences most frequently committed: vandalism, fare evasion, buying or selling stolen goods, driving without a licence, fights and riots, carrying a weapon and cannabis use. Far more boys than girls are involved, and school failure, low parental supervision and weak bonds with school are strongly associated with offending (Ruxton, 1996, pp. 229–302). The differences come in responses to crime.

The age of responsibility is lowest in Ireland at 7, followed by Scotland and Northern Ireland at 8, and England and Wales at 10. In the Netherlands and Greece it is 12, in France 13, in Austria, Germany and Italy 14, in Denmark, Finland and Sweden 15, in Spain and Portugal 16, and in Belgium and Luxembourg 18 (*ibid.*, p. 306). (See Chapter 1.)

Not only is the age of responsibility different but legal systems, as we have seen, are founded on different principles. The inquisitorial Napoleonic system (in France and Italy) is loosely associated with the welfare model, emphasizing informal court proceedings and judicial discretion to decide on individualized, often educative measures. By contrast, the adversarial Roman system is associated more with a justice model, with clearly specified legal safeguards for the defendant and a case which must be proven, and then responded to with determinate and proportional penalties. Countries with this model tend to have a lower age of responsibility (Ruxton, 1996, p. 306).

The welfare approach means in practice a range of social work measures to help the young person. Continental Europe has a wider range of professions here than the UK, typically with family social workers in the casework tradition, and then an educative/pedagogical strand of social work which works directly with young people, often in groups. Social pedagogy requires as much as four years of university education, and especially in the northern countries there is much higher status in working with children and young people, whether in residential or community settings, than we find in the UK. In these countries there is a concern that juvenile incarceration should be limited and short term, and directed towards rehabilitation; that custody should where possible be kept for the most serious offences and wherever possible combined with weekend leaves and so forth. All in all, the UK and Ireland are exceptions here, sending 'a vastly greater proportion of young people to prison than any other state in the EU' (Ruxton, 1966, p. 313).

Conclusion

While I have tried to bring out some of the positive developments in policies and services which affect children in the EU, there are worrying signs for children in the EU and beyond. Children have become a smaller part of the population and one which is less powerful in the struggle for resources in marketized welfare systems. The relative decline in the position of children, in their economic status, health and general welfare, has been dramatically described in the UNICEF report 'Children at Risk in Central and Eastern Europe' (1997). Only the Scandinavian countries of the EU have consistently tried to develop services and policies predicated on children's interests and needs; elsewhere their welfare is seen through and subsumed by family and labour market policies. Nevertheless, even in non-Scandanavian countries, for instance Germany, there are examples of imaginative approaches to childhood, responding to the social isolation of and environmental threats to children with democratic and flexible community services. The creation of coherent, integrated and flexible early-years services is a task which many British local authorities have set themselves, and there are innovative approaches to be found in many EU countries. But their further development and implementation requires a societal responsibility to children and childhood to parallel the contemporary rhetoric about parental responsibility (Moss and Petrie, 1997). As we have seen, countries vary in their understanding of such responsibilities and in their commitment to supporting them.

References

Bradshaw, J., Ditch, J., Holmes, H. and Whiteford, P. (1993a) Support for children: a comparison of arrangements in fifteen countries. London: HMSO.

Bradshaw, J., Ditch, J., Holmes, H. and Whiteford, P. (1993b) A comparative study of child support in fifteen countries. *Journal of European Social Policy*, 3 (4), 255–71.

Cannan, C. (1996) Social development with children and families in France. In C. Cannan and C. Warren (eds), *Social Action with Children and Families*. London: Routledge.

Cohen, B. (1995) Children and families and the 1996 inter-governmental conference. *Social Work in Europe*, 2 (3), 41–2.

Cohen, B. and Hagen, U. (1997) Children's services: shaping up for the millennium – supporting children and families in the UK and Scandinavia. Edinburgh: Children in Scotland.

Colla-Müller, H. (1993) Germany. In M.J. Colton and W. Hellinckx (eds), *Child Care in the EC: A Country-Specific Guide to Foster and Residential Care*. Aldershot: Arena.

Colton, M. and Hellinckx, W. (1994) Residential and foster care in the European Community: current trends in policy and practice. *British Journal of Social Work*, 24, 559–76.

Cooper, A. and Hetherington, R. (1995) *Positive Child Protection: A View from abroad*. Lyme Regis: Russell House Press.

Ditch, J., Barnes, H., Bradshaw, J. and Eardley, T. (1996a) A synthesis of national family policies 1994. European Observatory on National Family Policies, Commission of the European Communities (DGV)/ University of York.

Ditch, J., Barnes, H., Bradshaw, J. and Eardley, T. (1996b) Developments in national family policies in 1994. European Observatory on National

Family Policies, Commission of the European Communities/University of York.

European Commission (DG-V) (1994) The European Union and the Family. Social Europe supplement 1/94, Brussels.

European Commission Network on Child Care (1996a) 1986–1996: a decade of achievements. Brussels: European Commission.

European Commission Network on Child Care (1996b) Quality targets in services for young children, Brussels: European Commission.

Evans, M. (1996) *Families on the Dole in Britain, France and Germany.* London: London School of Economics and Political Science.

Gerzer-Sass, A. and Pettinger, R. (1996) New social networks for families and children in Germany. In C. Cannan and C. Warren (eds), *Social Action with Children and Families.* London: Routledge.

Hantrais, L. (1995) *Social Policy in the European Union.* Basingstoke: Macmillan.

Hantrais, L. (1996) France: squaring the welfare triangle. In V. George and P. Taylor-Gooby (eds), *European Welfare Policy.* Basingstoke: Macmillan.

Hobcraft, J. and Kiernan, K. (1995) *Becoming a Parent in Europe.* London: London School of Economics and Political Science.

Kamerman, S.B. and Kahn, A.J. (1995) Innovations in toddler day care and family support services: an international overview. *Child Welfare,* **74** (6), 1281–1300.

Lawson, R. (1996) Germany: maintaining the middle way. In V. George and P. Taylor-Gooby (eds), *European Welfare Policy.* Basingstoke: Macmillan.

Lorenz, W. (1991) The new German Children and Young People's Act. *British Journal of Social Work,* **21,** 329–39.

Luckock, B., Volgar, R. and Keating, H. (1996) Child protection in France and England: authority, legalism and social work practice. *Child and Family Law Quarterly,* **8** (4), 297–311.

Madge, N. (1994) *Children and Residential Care in Europe.* London: National Children's Bureau.

Millar, J. and Warman, A. (1996) Family Obligations in Europe. London: Family Policy Studies Centre.

Moss, P. and Petrie, P. (1997) Children's services: time for a new approach. University of London, Institute of Education.

Qvortrup, J. (1995) Childhood and modern society: a paradoxical relationship? In J. Brannen and M. O'Brien (eds), *Childhood and Parenthood.* London: University of London, Institute of Education.

Ruxton, S. (1996) Children in Europe. London: NCH Action for Children.

Therborn, G. (1996) Child politics, dimensions and perspectives. *Childhood: A Global Journal of Child Research,* **3** (17), 29–44.

UNICEF (1997) Children at Risk in Central and Eastern Europe: Perils and Promises. Florence: International Child Development Centre.

PART 2

The Impact of Current Policy

5

The challenge of children in the education system

Margaret Maden

The school is the one public institution that all but a handful of children experience. In England and Wales, just over 7 per cent of children attend private (or 'independent') schools and around 0.5 per cent of children are educated at home. It is, therefore, the institutional process of *schooling* that is a statutory requirement and to opt out of this is a minority activity.

Schools represent, transmit and sometimes challenge a dense and complex conflation of social and educational history, as well as current expectations and norms. 'Where the rubber hits the road' is a telling and vivid American expression of this relationship. Schools are where society's hopes and fears are concentrated and synthesized into a detailed set of daily transactions involving all our children.

To put the matter more pedantically and accurately, however, most children spend around 15,000 hours in school between the ages of 4 and 16, the statutory ages between which school attendance is a legal requirement in England and Wales. This amounts to less than 15 per cent of children's lives, or some 23 per cent of their waking hours.

It is important, however, that the influences and forces acting on children's education outside the boundaries and capability of schools are not ignored. In their eagerness to reform and improve schools, governments frequently marginalize these wider forces. This is partly because over the past two decades academic studies in the UK and elsewhere have persuaded governments that the effect and impact of schools working with very similar children are dissimilar. Life chances (measured and described mainly through academic scores and outcomes) are thus observably affected by the *particular* school attended, irrespective of its budget, the age and condition of its buildings or, it appears, the experience and qualifications of its teachers. Pressure, then, is exerted on schools to improve rather than there being an emphasis on strategies which might improve the wider context of children's lives.

A huge literature is now available on 'school effect' and its less well understood or documented progeny, 'school improvement'. In most of this we should note that as energetic activity and centralized prescription increase, so, simultaneously, does an almost wilful dislocation and decoupling occur between the lived experiences and habitats of children and the directions taken in education policy. Thus it is that what is taught in schools and, increasingly, how it is taught are determined by central government, but in arriving at such decisions – affecting 7 million pupils in 25,000 primary and secondary schools in England and Wales – little or no reference is made to the wider experiences and lives of children.

No one should doubt governments' determined commitment to raising educational standards and to the importance ascribed to schools in securing the UK's success in the global economy. Within this there is an assumed and implicit concern for children, but no articulation of policy in relation to an analysis of their changing lives, needs and desires.

Who then are these children in the final years of this second millennium? What do we know about them, both inside and outside school? Some key UK statistical indicators (OPCS, 1993; Childline, 1997; NCH, 1998; Leffert and Petersen, 1995; Ghate and Daniels, 1997) include the following:

- In families with dependent children, 60% of couples are both in paid employment, with most women being in part-time jobs.
- The percentage of children under age 16 being brought up by lone parents has increased from 8% in 1972 to 21% in 1994.
- Half of all 21- to 24-year-olds are still living at home and the percentage of 16-year-olds moving from school to employment has fallen from 57 to 7 in the past fifteen years.
- Two hundred thousand young people living in the outer rings of major cities are not in education, training or employment and have no stable place to live or viable income.
- In 1995 some 3000 10-year-olds contacted Childline. Bullying and physical abuse accounted for 20% of the concerns, followed by family tensions and conflicts. Half said they had unsuccessfully tried to obtain advice and support elsewhere.
- Twenty-four per cent of households with dependent children have personal computers, 77% have video recorders and 91% have telephones. The proportion of 14- and 15-year-olds who watch more than three hours of television per evening has fallen from a third to a fifth between 1987 and 1997.
- During the same decade, more homework appears to be set and accomplished. For boys, an increase from 57 to 68% is recorded, for girls the increase is from 65 to 74%.
- In a survey of 8- to 15-year-olds carried out by the National Society for the Prevention of Cruelty to Children (NSPCC), 44% of the older

children in this group said that their greatest source of anxiety was their academic work. More generally, over 20% said they felt they had 'no one to turn to' about their worries.

- In the same survey, over three-quarters of children said their grandparents were important people in their lives, particularly so when (which was the case in a quarter of all homes surveyed) there was an absent parent.
- Almost half of all 12- to 19-year-olds, and 62% of 12- to 15-year-olds believe in God (though not necessarily the Christian one).
- Nearly 40% of 11- to 16-year-olds have part-time jobs and these include one in four under-13s who are, by law, barred from any kind of paid employment.
- One in five girls under age 16 claim to have experienced sexual intercourse, compared to almost one-third of boys.
- 'Teenage mothers' under the age of 15 have increased from 199 (1983), to 279 (1994) and in the 15-19 age group the increase is from 53,860 to 73,814.
- Sixty per cent of 11-year-olds express 'considerable concern' about their employment prospects and two-thirds express concern about 'the environment'.
- Among 15- and 16-year-olds, the reported use of drugs between 1989 and 1996 increased from 15% to 40% (cannabis), 2% to 20% (glues and solvents), 0.5% to 1% (heroin) and from 1% to 13% (amphetamines).
- Sixty per cent of 12- to 15-year-olds report themselves as having had at least one alcoholic drink in the previous week, but over the past decade the percentage of 'regular teenage drinkers' has declined.
- A quarter of 14- and 15-year-old boys and a third of girls are 'regular cigarette smokers'.
- Criminal convictions, mainly for theft and handling stolen goods, among 10- to 13-year-old boys fell from 3.8% in 1985 to 2.6% in 1994, but for girls rose from 1.1% to 2.3%.
- The highest level of respect accorded to adults is to parents (84%), police (56%) and teachers (55%), with MPs scoring just 8% and the royal family, 15%.
- The number of children living in families dependent on basic welfare benefit has doubled in the past ten years. The value or spending power of these benefits has fallen.
- Children in benefit-dependent families change school more often, lose more days of schooling through illness and are more likely to truant than their peers whose families are in paid employment.
- In LEAs with the highest levels of social and economic disadvantage, 20% of 16-year-olds left school with no graded examination results, compared with an English average of 9%.

- Almost a third of 12- to 19-year-olds acknowledged, in themselves, a degree of racial prejudice, compared with 40% of adults.
- Eighty per cent of children reported bullying at school and had already been the victim of at least one crime outside school.
- A third of 11- to 15-year-olds have played truant at least once, but only 3% regularly abscond.
- More than 75% of school-leavers who have been in the care of local authorities (around 8000 per annum) have no academic qualifications and most will be unemployed and not in education or training. More than half of school pupils in care regularly truant.
- In 1996 the achievements of girls in both GCSE and A-level examinations outstripped those of their male counterparts. In the 1950s twice as many boys as girls obtained at least one GCE 'O' level pass (equivalent to GCSE Grades A–C). Over the same period the proportion of female undergraduates has risen from under 10% to just over 50% of all UK university entrants. (Bedell, 1996)

Of course, these snatched and disconnected glimpses of children cannot tell us enough about our chosen subject. For this we need some closely observed studies, probably from a latter-day Turgenev or George Eliot. It is interesting, and unsurprising, that the compulsive surveying of children's attitudes and lives is three times as frequent for the over-13s as for the younger age group. This is probably because adults feel more threatened, provoked and bemused by 'teenagers'.

But whether by means of social attitude surveys or through the experienced and empathetic eye of a good teacher or imaginative novelist, we need a properly grounded knowledge of children before we implement, wholesale, large-scale educational reforms. The waves of such reform, year on year, from 1987 through to 1998 and beyond are not, however, characterized by any such knowledge. The adult view of what children should be and should learn is certainly evident; adults in positions of social and economic authority clearly express their quite legitimate expectations of children. However, it is odd that such expectations and provisions are not calibrated against any working hypothesis relating to the present condition of children.

From the surveys and polls of children conducted in recent years, from which the earlier listing of extracts and sound-bites has been drawn, it is possible to sketch such a working hypothesis. While an amalgam or composite picture is not possible or desirable, it is at least worth flagging a few salient characteristics. Children in contemporary Britain are, for example, more adult in terms of much of their behaviour and thinking than many 'official adults' choose to believe. Many children have to carry considerable domestic, social and financial responsibilities. Many children know more about drugs, crime, low-paid occupations (including many jobs in the 'black economy') and computers than do their parents and teachers.

The educational changes brought about by the Education Reform Act of 1988 started with the distribution of consultation papers in the school holidays of August 1987, trading under a cosy-sounding acronym, GERBIL (Great Education Reform Bill). The main elements started with a strongly centralized, prescribed National Curriculum for all state schools, and 'four key stages' extending from 5-year-old children to young men and women at age 16. Built into a densely packed curriculum were a series of assessments and tests to be applied at the end of each key stage, the results of which, for each school, would be published in so-called league tables. Additionally, a new school inspection system replaced the traditional Her Majesty's Inspectorate (HMI) and local education authority (LEA) inspection teams. Under a new regulatory quango, the Office for Standards in Education (OFSTED), schools would be inspected every four years. The published reports of these inspections would also guide parents in their choice of school, and both would keep teachers 'on their toes' and sensitize them to the not-so-hidden hand of competition.

These reports and league tables were part of the government's strategy to inform parents about successful and less successful schools, in order that a quasi-marketplace, within which parents could exercise choice, could operate. A mixed outcome was apparently intended; schools exposed as less successful or downright diabolical would strive to improve, thus raising standards overall, or they would simply close down because of lack of custom.

Two related measures buttressed this marketplace. Every child now had a price tag or age-weighted pupil unit (AWPU) attached to them. The school was primarily funded (up to least 80% of its total budget) by the AWPU value for each child who attended the school. The value of an 8-year-old might be £1300, while £1800 would be claimed for a 15-year-old. Second, a school could simply 'opt out' of an LEA if it felt that the LEA was too 'controlling' or wedded to priorities which the school opposed. The way the LEA spent the residual funds it retained for wider educational purposes beyond the level of the individual school might also prompt a school to 'opt out' and take its nominal share of such centrally retained funds. Such 'wider purposes' included advisory teachers and inspectors, county youth orchestras, and development grants for small sixth forms, or for small Primary school clusters. Such 'opted-out' schools were called *grant-maintained schools* (GMS), and although there were few of them (under 18% of all secondary schools and 3% of all primary schools), the financial effects of their departure on the large majority of remaining schools were disproportionately damaging.

Such damage, combining financial hurt with marketplace conflict and competition, was much in evidence elsewhere in the educational system.

The behaviour of public institutions, from nursery schools to universities, changed – and was meant to. Year-on-year financial squeezes inevitably affected behavioural standards and norms, but except by virtue of random anecdote and staffroom gossip, these changes were rarely investigated from the point of view of children and young people. The balance sheet, weighing greater educational participation and 'entitlement' against greater selectivity and exclusion in some parts of the system, still needs to be assayed.

Also affecting schools and children were reforms in further and higher education. Largely because of the 'poll tax' fiasco, the government suddenly removed further education (FE) and sixth-form colleges from LEA control in 1992. This reduced, at a stroke, £2000 million from local authority expenditure, thus making more manageable the new council tax arrangements. A new quango (the Further Education Funding Council) was established so that FE colleges could be centrally funded on a formula of Chinese complexity. Whether the effect was intended or not, significant areas of college work, especially for students with learning difficulties, were suddenly under-funded or, in the case of non-vocational leisure and 'hobbies' courses, not funded at all. Competition between colleges, and between schools and colleges, for 16- to 18-year-old 'customers' rapidly took off. Benefit rule changes led to young people having to rely on parental support or part-time employment in order that their studies could be sustained, and in many cases the poorest students were simply unable to enrol or remain at college.

Meanwhile, as LEAs were being badly affected by their own year-on-year budget reductions and no longer had direct responsibility for further education, they implemented cuts in transport and maintenance grants for post-16 students. This was especially damaging for poorer students, and the damage was made worse if they attended colleges some distance from their home or if they needed to buy specialist equipment and clothing in, for example, catering, agriculture and music courses. Simultaneously, most local authorities reduced their youth service provision, and in this way, vital areas of support and development for 8- to 18-year-olds outside school or college hours simply disappeared.

Maintenance grants for university undergraduates remained mandatory, while they had always been discretionary, as well as minuscule, for 16- to 18-year-olds or adults on sub-degree courses. However, from 1990, student loans were introduced on a tapering-up basis, initially to augment the mandatory state grant to all undergraduates, except those whose parents were means-tested at a sufficiently high level to exclude them from eligibility. Starting at the equivalent to 15% of the maximum grant available, the loan reached a 50:50 position in 1995/96. Since then, legislation has been introduced so that, in 1998, undergraduates will be required to contribute towards their tuition fees, as well as to their own maintenance costs.

Across the education system, public expenditure rose inexorably during the 1980s and 1990s. Conservative Chancellors and Secretaries of State reminded Parliament of this fact on a regular basis, as will, undoubtedly, their Labour successors. However, the units of resource, or expenditure per student, fell. This was because more and more young people chose to continue their education at the end of their statutory schooling at age 16, rising from 38 to 68% during the eighteen years of Conservative rule. Likewise, the proportion of 18- and 19-year-olds proceeding to university almost doubled during the same period to around 35%. Hence, educational productivity increased as more and more pupils and students participated and acquired qualifications, but cost much less on a per capita basis. This was achieved through a range of measures: larger teaching groups, more technology, less 'contact time' (especially for counselling and broader academic tutoring support) in higher and further education. In schools, absolute cuts in budgets resulted in increased class sizes, fewer subject options in the senior reaches of secondary schools, reduced spending on books, cheaper school meals and so on. In all sectors – schools, colleges and universities – 'downsizing' took a grip. Reduced staffing on permanent contracts, with increased use of fixed-term contracts and, therefore, much lower 'on costs' for staff training entitlements, pensions and sickness pay became ubiquitous features of all educational establishments, and of LEAs.

How such radical reforms and changes have affected the ultimate customer, the learner, has yet to be assessed. While the high-stake indicators remain encouraging, in terms of increased educational participation (with an uncomfortable downwards 'blip' in 16-year-old enrolments in 1996), it is too early to know whether this is a permanent cultural shift, denoting a growing allegiance to a 'learning society', or a shorter-term response to high levels of unemployment. If the latter are endemic, then perhaps the former is a corresponding reaction – one which is both utilitarian *and* a vote of confidence in the education system.

It is more important, however, to examine the extent to which children and young people *do* derive satisfaction and have their learning needs met in schools, colleges and universities. The rhetoric of government and other policy-makers is that nothing less than a mass education system serving the needs of all children (and adults) will suffice. In this sense, the achievement of ambitious national targets depends on a more complete understanding of children and young people than policy-makers and providers currently possess. They would do well to note that there are already indicative signs of stress and strain emerging. Equally, there is evidence of good practice, where children are well served across a wide range of their needs in schools and in other parts of the education system. Both negative and positive indicators and exemplars need to be acknowledged and learned from by policy-makers.

In recent years there has been a steadily growing practice in many schools of sampling pupil attitudes. In 1989, one of my predecessors at Keele University, Professor Tim Brighouse, established the Centre for Successful Schools and, within that framework, worked with colleagues in the university, in schools and in LEAs to produce attitude survey questionnaires for pupils and parents. The analysis of these is carried out by the Centre for Successful Schools, and each school or LEA is also provided with comparative data from a wider national database. More and more schools continue to use this system to help them identify organizational strengths and weaknesses which appear to matter to pupils.

This kind of inquiry is part of a growing concern about the remoteness of much educational reform at macro and meta levels. 'What would happen', ask Fullan and Stiegelbauer (1991, p. 170), 'if we treated the student as someone whose opinion mattered?' Nieto (1994, pp. 395–6) suggests that:

> Reforming school structures alone will not lead to differences in student achievement . . . if such changes are not accompanied by profound changes in how we as educators think about our students. One way to begin the process of changing school policies is to listen to students' views about them.

Professor Michael Barber's summary of the Keele data (1994) concluded that 'the findings do not make pretty reading and the results demand a national focus on the issue of pupil motivation in secondary education'. He first, though, stresses the broadly positive findings, which include the following.

- 88 per cent of pupils are usually happy at school;
- 70 per cent say they work as hard as they can;
- over 90 per cent believe that their school work is important;
- 70 per cent of pupils get on well with most or all of their teachers;
- when asked whether the school and they are like good friends, friends, distant relatives, strangers or enemies, over 50 per cent place school in the first two categories, with another quarter choosing 'distant relatives'. Only 10 per cent choose 'strangers' and 6% 'enemies'.

Barber (1994, pp. 1–2) identifies the less encouraging aspects of the pupil attitude database and concludes that

> for many young people in the UK school, particularly the secondary phase, fails to inspire . . . Schools vary greatly but there is a national pattern in which as many as 17 per cent of Year 10 (14- to 15-year-olds) truant, on their own admission, 'sometimes' or 'often'. Among Year 11 pupils the equivalent figure is 20%. A third of pupils state that other pupils in their classes disrupt lessons

every day, and in Year 11, the year that pupils take the GCSEs, 92 per cent of pupils state that other pupils in their classes disrupt them sometimes or even more regularly.

The database also confirms the existence of a huge range of schools in terms of how pupils experience them. More recent analysis of the Keele data shows that in 'best-case' schools, for example, the proportion of pupils claiming that other pupils disrupt their learning 'on a daily basis' is 6% of the cohort. The 'worst-case' equivalent is 66%. In a fairly typical 'shire county', its 40 secondary schools show a range from 20 to 45% on this same question.

Likewise, in the same LEA, the range of pupils who claim to be the victims of persistent bullying extends from 3% to 14% of the cohort. This compares with a database average of 6% and provides just one more piece of evidence for schools and LEAs to use as a measure of school ethos.

In this same, most recent report on the database, we are also told that the

> broad areas we have identified in which the pupils express very real concerns about their schooling, and which undoubtedly influence their motivation and their approach to study, include:
> • feeling that it is not legitimate to want to learn and discuss their learning with their peers
> • having time and opportunity – at lunchtime or after school – to 'catch up' on missed work
> • having access to teachers – at lunchtime or after school – to ask about things they do not understand but know are important
> • receiving irrelevant or 'unprepared' homework tasks
> • managing the multiple demands of homework, course-work and revision
> • finding time to discuss their learning with their teacher(s)
> • not understanding how to proceed when told to 'work hard' or 'work harder'
> • being helped to 'explore' standards for judging the quality of their work in different subjects
> • not having access to the necessary books and equipment to do their work.
> (Barber, 1994, pp. 1–2)

Understandably, the schools who use these pupil attitude data to inform their own improvement strategies emphasize their success in increasing the percentage of pupils who express positive attitudes to school. All well and good, but this may obscure the alienation from the mainstream of a smaller group of pupils.

The Keele data indicate that 'a few individuals' amounts to a significant minority nationally, with consequent policy implications, as well as serious problems encountered by them, and because of them, in any particular school. There are signs that because of the government's 'academic pressure' exerted on schools (and, in turn, on pupils by schools), in order that the measured outcomes of the majority are improved, there is less attention given to the 'intractable few'.

In some parts of the inner city and in large out-of-town post-war housing estates, it is known that over a quarter of 14- and 15-year-olds have either voted with their feet or colluded with their teachers and have stopped attending school. The drawn-out and costly procedures involved in persuading them back to school and, equally difficult, persuading their parents that this is something that is desirable and feasible, often results in no official or legal action being taken.

Other pupils are excluded by the school either for a fixed term of one or two weeks or permanently. In the latter case, it is the LEA that is responsible for their education in a variety of Pupil Referral Units (PRUs) or, as they are more commonly called, 'sin bins'. Since 1991, there has been a 50% increase in school exclusions. These account for only 1% (11,000) of all schoolchildren, 83% of whom are from secondary schools, 13% from primary and 4% from special schools.

Research into excluded children reveals that they are likelier to be male, with special educational needs, underachieving, large for their age, new to the school and with few or no friends, low in self-esteem, black or of mixed race and with high levels of hyperactivity. The stress factors which make exclusion more likely include:

- family breakdown
- time in care/social work involvement
- disability/bereavement
- violence/abuse
- major accident/incident
- police/courts involvement/substance misuse
- special educational needs statement
- no member of household in paid work.

These are the children who are among those who are not being well served by the school system and, in the particular case of excluded pupils, are costing the public sector some £10,500 per annum, as opposed to an average of £2500 when in school.

Just under 10 per cent of all 16-year-olds leave school (and 'leave' is what they do, if they have not already done so years before) without any graded examination results. Most of this group are not entered for GCSE or other examinations; only a very small minority of pupils actually submit themselves for assessment, then fail to be graded. It is almost certainly the case that the insistent orthodoxy pressed on, and promoted by, most schools is sharply at odds with the needs of this marginally growing minority. A minority of more than 10 per cent is not only an expensive failure in terms of opportunity costs for them, their families and the rest of us (throughout their lives), it also denotes the serious limitations of an essentially Fordist model of schooling.

Hence, we now have an increasingly orthodox model of schooling, aided and abetted by the National Curriculum and reduced variety and choice between different examination boards responsible for administering GCSE and A-level syllabuses and exams. Such orthodoxy is further confirmed by OFSTED inspection criteria.

The challenges presented by this state of affairs are most evident for the dispossessed and alienated 12–15 per cent, who are frequently disadvantaged socially and economically as well. They are often, but not invariably, in schools deemed by OFSTED to have 'serious weaknesses' or to be in need of 'special measures'. Additionally, 18 schools were named in May 1997, as New Labour assumed control of the Department for Education and Employment, as not having made sufficient progress since receiving a poor OFSTED report in the previous two years. They were almost all serving quite seriously damaged communities. An earlier report by former HMI and an eminent academic researcher had made it abundantly clear that the longer experience in New York City of 'naming and shaming' such schools was totally ineffective and made things worse rather than better. The immediate impact on students, their families and teachers, was especially counter-productive. An inter-agency, holistic strategy is needed in such cases, a strategy which includes, but does not isolate, education and schooling. The government's recent proposals for Education Action Zones, which are meant to bring together a range of public, private and voluntary agencies in a more integrated way, should be welcomed in this regard.

The increased conformity and standardization of schooling is a curious phenomenon in this post-Fordist age. It is all done in the name of raising standards and levels of achievement. Whether the standard model is the *optimal* model for the children and young people whose lives are sketched in the earlier part of this chapter is a beguiling question. Their demanding lives, their experiences and knowledge do not sit easily alongside a school system which so stresses conformity and rigidity. Some argue that by presenting, as they do, elements of structure and prescription to otherwise formless lives, these latter characteristics are exactly what are appreciated by third-millennium children.

However, these children are being prepared for a society that will be different, in terms of paid and unpaid employment, family structures and behaviour, cultural and ethnic diversity, from any that today's adults could ever have conceived possible when they were children. Is today's black T model Ford appropriate for such challenges?

Michael Barber, in his recent book *The Learning Game* (1996), suggests otherwise. His views are important, not least because of his current role in the Department for Education and Employment as the head of the new

Schools Standards and Effectiveness Unit. Barber argues that 'we need to redesign the whole process of learning'. He correctly questions our current orthodoxy:

> Is it sensible, for example, for secondary school pupils to charge round buildings, carrying their bags and jostling their peers as they dash from forty-five minutes of one subject to forty-five minutes of another? This bizarre dance governed by the insistent ringing of bells could not be created by anyone who started from the beginning – the learner – and focussed on the learning process. (p. 250)

and

> Pupils in our schools, for example, are grouped according to their age, but why? Learning is assumed to take place best when groups of around thirty pupils are put in one room with one teacher, but why? In spite of the explosion of learning opportunities, we still assume that a school – any school – can provide all the learning opportunities that any young person might seek, but why? And we could extend the list almost endlessly. If we seek to re-engineer education, these and other assumptions will have to be questioned and perhaps overturned. Rules are there to be broken. (p. 251)

Sadly, however, the policy pragmatist (or is it pessimist?) in Barber rejects all such questions and the more imaginative strategies he proposes in response to them. Instead, he appears to conclude that the 'conservatism of vested interests' and schools which are 'hidebound with tradition and still locked in the debates of yesteryear' render such fundamental reform unfeasible. His explicit support of, and executive involvement in, a New Labour government could be taken as a hopeful sign that a radical re-engineering strategy might emerge. Unfortunately, there is little to suggest that this is at all likely. Indeed, the government's hegemonic grip on everything conventional and conforming is dramatically evident at every turn: school uniforms today, phonics tomorrow, homework quotas next week. Detailed means, and not just strategic ends, are being willed and determined from Sanctuary Buildings (the headquarters of the Department for Education and Employment) on an hourly basis.

Just occasionally, we witness an illuminating flash of the new child in conflict with the new, strait-jacketed school. The inherent contradictions between recent educational reform and 'girl power' emerged in July 1997 when Sarah Briggs, a 15-year-old pupil in a Nottinghamshire school, was expelled because she had written to her local newspaper and complained about teacher absences in her school. The school did not deny the truth of her criticisms, but wrote to her parents and explained that the expulsion was because Sarah had been guilty of 'behaviour which brings the school into disrepute and [*sic*] could affect future pupil numbers'. In other words, the school's image in the new educational marketplace was seen to be more important than the substantive issues raised by a pupil – issues which directly affected the quality of teaching and learning.

Pupils must, indeed, be absorbing, at one level of consciousness or another, an array of messages about the new education 'marketplace'. While there is beginning to be a corpus of research knowledge about teacher stress and 'high-anxiety' behaviour when an OFSTED inspection is imminent, there is very little available in relation to pupils' perceptions and reactions to the same event. Collusion, between teachers and pupils, is a well-documented phenomenon when 'an inspector calls'. Less well observed or monitored is the effect on pupils when their teachers are so preoccupied – and deflected from their normal work – by OFSTED demands for detailed documentation from teachers. For between six and nine months, schools are building up to an OFSTED inspection which itself lasts for three to five days. The published report is added to the performance 'league' tables which rank the school's seeming effectiveness locally. Both are stressed as being of crucial importance to the school's reputation and image; the underlying message to teachers is often taken as being that 'your job is on the line'. How all of this reaches and affects pupils is worthy of proper study. Does the experience enhance the pupils' sense of formal education being a worthwhile activity? Does the experience increase the number of pupils who aspire to teaching as a career? What is the pupil's understanding of public accountability?

Other confusions and contradictions abound in this realm of adult messages to children. Not only in schools and colleges are there conflicting versions of the boundaries between childhood and adulthood and, most importantly, of the rite of passage between these two, never absolute, conditions. The status of children and young people is a paradoxical one in which they can, for example, pay taxes but not vote, drive cars but not rent one. Current educational policy in respect of league tables, annual assessments, minimum homework times, and partnerships between business and education add to these tensions.

Ann Oakley and Berry Mayall, writing in the *Guardian* 24 October 1996, raise related questions about current confusions and trends,

> A fundamental issue here is the status of children's rights. [Michael] Barber wants children to work not only during the day, but in the evening too, to make up the deficiencies of the state education system. He wants parents and teachers to collaborate in forcing children to conform to school agendas. Where in all this is the child as active learner as investigator, as partner with adults, in education? Where is the school as a democratic enterprise, enabling children to learn citizenship through participation? And where is the family as a democratic unit, with mothers and fathers equally responsible for what happens to their children?

It is hardly surprising that children and young people are often confused and perhaps rendered cynical by such contradictions and seeming hypocrisies. Michael Barber may be correct in his rather despairing assessment of the teaching profession as 'locked in the debates of yesteryear', but politicians also need to assume much of the responsibility for the messy situation in which children frequently find themselves. The uneasy stand-off between schools and the wider political–social nexus in drugs and sex education represents such dilemmas in a sharply delineated form. Regulations now limit and prescribe what is to be taught in these areas of human behaviour, areas of consuming interest to children. Governing bodies, as conduits between schools and their wider communities, have explicit powers and duties in shaping and authorizing the detail of what is taught. Parents, local business people and community representatives form the majority on each school's governing body and the headteacher is usually a member, as well as its main professional adviser. There is also growing evidence that teachers do not always possess up-to-date and accurate knowledge about AIDS and HIV, drugs (including tobacco), contraception and laws relating to sexual behaviour and drug abuse, for example. Further, and crucially, it is an area of the curriculum, both formal and informal, that requires an inter-agency approach. Health and police authorities, probation and social services, as well as a range of voluntary agencies, need to work with schools in order that these issues can be authentically and accurately discussed and taught. Yet the pushing of schools into a position of glorious (and competitive) isolation has had the opposite effect. Many young people know more (or certainly have reason to believe they know more) than the adults in their lives at school and at home about these matters.

On another issue of acute social concern in these latter years of this second millennium, a report of the National Commission of Inquiry into the Prevention of Child Abuse stated that

> whilst teachers are often very good at reporting concerns to their heads, developments in school management had made it more difficult to help children at risk. There has been a fragmentation of services in health and education. Under local management of schools it becomes more difficult for a school to budget for the prevention of child abuse.

The sharper focus on academic results which schools now have cannot, and should not, be spurned. Children are realistic about this and increasingly know what they want and expect from schools, even if they do not always get it. However, it is entirely counter-productive, and an instance of short-termism at its worst, to marginalize society's task in supporting the wider social and emotional aspects of growing up. Thus, the prevention of child abuse and the providing to children of a well-grounded education on matters of sexual behaviour, drugs abuse and related laws are clearly needed, and more besides. Whether it is for schools alone to respond to such needs is a separate matter.

Pugh and Rea Price (1995) have analysed and described the contradictory legislation of recent years, including the Children Act of 1989 and various Education Acts. They conclude the Education Acts have had a disabling effect on schools and local authorities in terms of schools' assumed responsibilities.

At the same time, the Audit Commission published *Misspent Youth* (1996), which demonstrates the extent to which public money is wasted by the lack of collaboration between agencies. It shows how a 20 per cent increase in the number of children cautioned rather than prosecuted would release £40 million for expanding preventive measures – measures which are at their most effective when schools, youth and probation services work together.

Taking such principles further, Tom Wylie, Chief Executive of the National Youth Agency, has spoken eloquently and sensibly about an 'agenda of social renewal: the achieving school; the empowering youth group; the inclusive community; the enabling state'. He goes on to argue for a youth policy, perhaps articulated in a Youth Charter, which would guarantee to young people

> the provision of a safe, warm, well-equipped meeting place within a bus ride; easy access to reliable information, planned opportunities to develop personal skills, opportunities to participate each month in drama, music, sport and voluntary action, a key worker to give support in a crisis, and a chance to make decisions about the local youth project and have a say on services which affect them through a youth forum. (*TES*, 20 June 1997)

As both Wylie, and Pugh and Rea Price have argued, there is a need for central, as well as local, government action. Pugh and Rea Price called for matched, related training programmes (and specific grants to pay for these) across education and social services in matters relating to the early detection and treatment of children with emotional and behavioural problems.

Whatever structure or mechanism is used and judged to be most efficacious, the main issues remain those of establishing policies which are rooted in a holistic view of children. It is convenient and manageable for adult professionals to act and think within the security of a specialist niche, be it schooling, youth justice or health. For children and, indeed, for most of us in our normal 'lay' lives, such segmentation is neither helpful nor realistic.

For the boy whose behaviour sparked off an unholy row between governors, parents and teacher members of the National Association of

Schoolmasters/Union of Women Teachers at Manton Junior School in Nottinghamshire, the lack of collaborative support from the education and social services arms of the same local authority was lamentable. Likewise, it was a 13-year-old girl whose pregnancy and challenging behaviour at the Ridings School in Halifax first gave teachers apparently legitimate cause to walk off the job. As this particular stone was unturned, it was clear that while strong and positive action was needed of an educational kind, social and economic intervention was also required.

It is wrong, however, to assume that in education, the challenge of children is entirely locked into circumstances of social and economic disadvantage. While it is true that integrated policies and co-ordinated action are especially important in such cases, there are wider challenges which extend beyond these. Aligning Michael Barber's analysis and questions about schools with the behaviour, attitudes and experiences we can observe among today's children inevitably leads to the conclusion that some fundamental re-engineering is needed.

Thinking along similar lines is the Organisation for Economic Co-operation and Development (OECD), which recently examined the educational and curricular challenges facing schools in 20 of its member states. It observes that:

> implications of the change from education of an elite to mass education are still being worked out, and as schools grapple with dealing with the whole range of society's needs, more seems to be expected of them as other institutions lose their influence. The lives of the young people in schools are also changing rapidly, at a pace and in ways which neither the school nor politicians are able to control. Thus, the expectations, the social and family pressures, and the means of support which mould the lives of pupils are all very different from those on which present school programmes were based. (OECD, 1994, p. 50)

Such observations have much in common with the findings of a recent DEMOS study group, which suggested that

> large numbers of school leavers and graduates are ill-prepared for the challenges and rigours of the world of work. Employers complain that, even if they have qualifications, they lack personal qualities – initiative, motivation, organisational skills. The changing nature of employment means that the challenge of employability is constantly shifting.
>
> We can sum up our concerns as follows: the formal education system cannot, on its own, produce rounded individuals who know themselves and those around them, and are capable of adapting to change with skill and confidence.

In both these studies, emphasis is placed on a wider range of learning contexts, beyond the nine to four school day and desk. As well as more bespoke educational programmes, frequently facilitated by a more imaginative use of information technology, there is an insistent call for more experiential learning. Hence, the OECD reports that

> increasingly, much vocational education occurs on working-sites; contextual learning as many business leaders call it. With the expansion of education for those for whom school environments are not conducive to learning this is important. It is important, too, to make available to schools a wider range of situation and of technology than they will be able to provide ... there is a lack of research and analysis on important ideas such as contextual learning or situational learning. Both these deserve more attention. (p. 34)

DEMOS, likewise, draws our attention to

> a remarkable growth of community-based learning initiatives, in particular, those which create opportunities for young people themselves actively to lead, manage and take responsibility for the projects in which they are involved.

In such ways can the motivation and engagement of children and young people be developed and sustained. The waxing and waning of learners' capacity to fully concentrate and acquire knowledge and skills (especially during adolescence) will be best served by a more flexible, post-Fordist school system. Additionally, the growing body of knowledge about the variable aspects or kinds of intelligence, put forward by Howard Gardner, renders obsolete the standardized learning package. It also renders obsolete the present government's belief in the value of 'streaming' of children in schools, according to some immutable measurement of their 'general ability'.

For many children, most of the time, they need to be able to adjust parts of their learning programmes, sometimes on to 'fast forward', sometimes on to 'replay' and sometimes on to 'freeze frame'. (Don't we all?) Barber's questioning of our grouping of pupils according to age is an associated feature of a quite counter-productive rigidity in the way we organize schools and education. It is also a feature of an unfortunate tendency to infantilize the education of children. Schools and schooling are the critical, high-investment means by which we provide our children with formal education. There are competing claims and values in all of this, as well as contradictory demands and assertions. These claims, values, demands and assertions are of the adult world, especially that part which looks back longingly to its own, usually mythical, 'golden age'.

What is needed is a thoroughgoing needs analysis which reflects and represents who children are, their lived experience, their expectations and aspirations in the next millennium, as well as now. The futures thinking of Barber, Wylie, the OECD and DEMOS, touched on in this chapter, has to be assimilated and aligned with such a needs analysis and a mental model of the actuality of children. Their challenge is both to us and, of course, from us.

Education reforms of the past decade have been strong on society's challenging children but have elided children's challenges to society. Reforms have also taken too much for granted, not least the passivity and acquiescence of children. Such assumptions might appear to have been justified, but we would be wrong to believe that children fail to observe and absorb, at a quite deep level, the behaviour of adults. Thus, it is the so-called hidden curriculum of schools and colleges which also has to be thought about. The increased numbers of teachers on short-term contracts, the fretful displacement activities of teachers responding to 'new management' or to external inspection systems, the high-gloss, high-expenditure marketing strategies of many schools and colleges – these need to be evaluated and thought about from the point of view of pupils and students. Experiential learning, after all, takes place in unintended as well as intended ways.

Nonetheless, the plus side of our current situation includes a massive enlargement of enrolled, participating young people in formal education, following the end of statutory schooling. Equally, we actually know quite a lot about children and young people, and much of it is encouraging and impressive. We also have some excellent models of innovatory practice, sometimes no more than glimpses, from the UK and from other countries, which point the way forward towards a more flexible, bespoke form of schooling.

What we do not yet have is a public strategy that rests on empirically based knowledge of children and their real lives, or ways of learning which treat children as more than potentially fractious dependants. In other words, public policy in education still has to acknowledge and use the knowledge that exists concerning children's lives, their multiple intelligences and the variable, flexible structures which are most likely to maximize learning outcomes. Such outcomes are more than academic, as are the conditions which are needed if continuous and successful learning is to be nourished in all, not just some of, our young people.

References

Audit Commission (1996) *Misspent Youth: Young People and Crime.* London: Audit Commission.

Barber, M. (1994) *Young People and Their Attitudes to School.* Keele: Department of Education, Keele University.

Barber, M. (1996) *The Learning Game.* London: Gollancz.

Bentley, T. (1997) *Learning Beyond the Classroom*. London: DEMOS.

ChildLine (1997) *Beyond the Limit: Children Who Live With Parental Alcohol Misuse*. London: ChildLine.

Fullan, M. and Steigelbauer, S. (1991) *The New Meaning of Educational Change*. London: Cassell.

Gardner, H. (1993) *The Unschooled Mind: How Children Think and How Schools Should Teach*. London: HarperCollins.

Ghate, D. and Daniels, A. (1997) *Talking About My Generation*. London NSPCC.

Leffert, N. and Petersen, A.C. (1995) Patterns of development in adolescence. In M. Rutter and D.J. Smith (eds), *Psycho-social Disorders in Young People: Time Trends and their Causes*. Chichester: Wiley.

Nieto, S. (1994) Lessons from students on creating a chance to dream. *Harvard Educational Review*, 64(4), 392–426.

NSPCC (1996) Report of the National Commission of Inquiry into the Prevention of Child Abuse. London: NSPCC.

Pugh, G. and Rea Price, J. (1995) Championing Children: A Report on Manchester City Council Services for Children. Manchester: City Council.

Smith, T. and Noble, M. (1995) *Education Divides: Poverty and Schooling in the 1990s*. London: C.P.A.G.

TUC (1997) *Working Classes: A Report on School-age Labour in England and Wales*. London: TUC.

Wiley, T. (1996) Setting Priorities for a Coherent Youth Policy. *Policy Update, Issue 6*. Leicester: National Youth Agency.

6

The health care system and children

Zarrina Kurtz

The requirement for children to flourish and grow up in good health brings significant challenges to any health care system. This is particularly clear if health is defined as it was in the constitution of the World Health Organization in 1946, as 'a state of complete mental, physical and social well-being, and not merely the absence of disease'. Since the introduction, at the same time, of the National Health Service in Britain, the pattern of ill health in children has undergone enormous changes, accompanied by a significant growth in knowledge and in the available technologies in health care. Parallel changes in our understanding and perception of childhood have also altered perceptions of what many problems mean in terms of the health of children, bringing further challenges to health policy and health care practice (Qvortrup, 1993). That all these changes have not been matched by comparable changes in the health care system has led to a degree of failure in effectively meeting children's needs for present and future health – and this presents challenges to children.

Outline of the health services for children and young people

Under the National Health Service (NHS) Act of 1946, British children of all ages became entitled to free health services. The Act established a tripartite health service such as had grown up previously: community health services provided by local authorities for children in school, children under the age of 5 and for expectant mothers; general medical services provided for the listed patients of independently contracted general practitioners; and specialist health services for all, provided in hospitals (Department of Health and Social Security et al., 1976).

In the 50 years since its inception, the NHS has undergone a number of major reforms. Recently, the way in which health care is planned and provided changed with the introduction of an internal market, as the result of the National Health Service and the Community Care Act of

1990. But many features of the services for children still reflect previous structures. A continuing separation between prevention and treatment is probably the most significant. Responsibility for prevention rests largely with the community services, which were taken on from local authorities by the NHS after the National Health Service Reorganisation Act 1973. (Primary prevention aims to prevent problems arising in the first place and is what is commonly meant by the term 'prevention'; secondary prevention aims to limit the duration of problems and the development of complications from a disorder; tertiary prevention is aimed at minimizing any handicap that may arise as a result of a disorder. Secondary and tertiary preventive measures can include treatment.) Meanwhile there was growing recognition of the fundamental part played by local authority services, notably social services and education, in the promotion of health and the prevention of illness (Department of Health and Social Security *et al.*, 1976; Audit Commission, 1994; Lindstrom and Spencer, 1995). While treatment for acute conditions and episodes remains hospital-based, the ongoing management of many problems is increasingly carried out by the community child health services and by primary care. Primary care is also responsible for many of the preventive services (Royal College of General Practitioners, 1982; Butler, 1989). The White Paper on the new NHS (Department of Health, 1997) and the Green Paper on public health (Department of Health, 1998) promise further structural changes, and together seek to establish a holistic approach to health, with health action zones and health improvement programmes closely related to primary and community health services. What impact these proposed changes will have remains to be seen. Furthermore, in England and Scotland, the proposed restructuring of primary and community care aims to give these services even greater authority and responsibility for determining patterns of patient care.

In the internal health care market, child health services, like services for all groups in the population, are commissioned by each health authority in England and Wales in the light of an assessment of the needs of their resident populations, although this function may be taken on by a larger number of primary care groups when the White Paper proposals are implemented. The services are delivered to members of the population by providers which include hospitals, specialist units, community clinics and general practices. Commissioning is essentially a strategic exercise which determines what services are purchased by the health authority from providers. Purchasing is achieved by means of several mechanisms, including contracts for specified services which are negotiated between the purchaser and the provider. It should be noted that under the new government White Paper, annual contracts are to be replaced by long-term service agreements with quality standards. Services for children are likely to be purchased from several providers, often including both a

Hospital Trust delivering acute services (usually a hospital) and a Community Trust. Services of a specialist nature, such as cancer treatment or heart surgery, are usually purchased by means of separate contracts with specialist centres, which may or may not be part of a trust providing more general children's services, or within the health authority's own boundary (examples are listed at 3.37 in Department of Health, 1991). Services are sometimes required for a child whose needs cannot be met by a provider with which the purchaser has an established contract. Examples include treatments for rare genetic conditions and for severe and complicated manifestations of a disorder, such as may occur in anorexia nervosa. These treatments, which tend to be expensive, may require what is termed an extra-contractual referral (ECR) to a specialist centre.

General practitioners (GPs) are independently contracted to the NHS – not to local health authorities – to provide certain services such as the Child Health Surveillance programme (National Health Service Management Executive, 1992). Certain general practitioners had become fund-holders (under the GP Contract 1990) and could purchase services directly from other providers. The extent to which fund-holding GPs were involved in local health strategy and purchasing decisions based on health authority commissioning was variable. Fund-holding, in any event, has been phased out and replaced by Primary Care Groups – eventually to become Trusts.

Providers of health services are not necessarily within the NHS. They include private and voluntary-sector organizations, which may offer a wide range of services, often of a highly specialized nature. Local authorities, because they have parental responsibility for some children (including due attention to their health care needs) also provide services such as respite care facilities. Local authorities also have a key role in relation to children with special needs such as those with learning difficulties. Apart from their purchasing arrangements with health authorities and with GPs, providers can have financial agreements and contracts with each other in order to secure certain elements of service, such as clinical psychology input to a specialist child and adolescent mental health team in one trust from the psychology department in another, or for social work expertise from the local social services.

Separation between the distinct functions of commissioning and providing is the essence of the internal market. Thus, having a champion for the needs of the local population, with the financial power to influence what and how services are provided to meet those needs, was one part of the twin vision for the 1990 NHS reforms. The other part was that competition between providers to attract funding would lead to greater value in the services provided, in terms of the effectiveness, cost and quality of health care. However, in the White Paper (Department of

Health, 1997), competition is to be replaced by co-operation and collaboration as the government believes that competition has had a largely negative effect. These functions (commissioning and providing) are closely linked in the way in which population 'needs' are defined: a need for health care must be associated with a known ability to benefit from a particular service (National Health Service Management Executive, 1993). Thus, the assessment of population needs is a means for making rationing decisions about the deployment of health care resources. Technically, these decisions require evidence about the ability to benefit (not only from the research evidence but also from national and local experts) as well as from users of services and their carers.

The main components of a full range of health services for children were set out by the Department of Health and endorsed in Health Service Guidelines HSG(91)1, as follows:

- primary care service for children and their families;
- comprehensive children's departments incorporating facilities for in-patients, day care, out-patients, treatment of accidents and emergencies and neonatal care;
- access to (tertiary) regional and supraregional specialities;
- community child health services for pre-school and school-aged children (with close, well-defined working arrangements with primary care and local authority services);
- child development centres for the assessment and monitoring of children with chronic illness and disability;
- health promotion programmes relevant to the needs of children and their families.

Major influences upon child health services

The same period since the Second World War that has seen the development of the National Health Service has seen a striking growth in knowledge about child development, health and disease, and in technologies that have greatly increased our understanding in this area and our ability to tackle poor health (Department of Health and Social Security *et al.*, 1976; National Children's Bureau, 1987; Forfar, 1988). One result has been the definition of child-specific health services (as distinct from maternal and infant provision), and the growth of the specialty of paediatrics. From the British Paediatric Association (previously affiliated to the Royal College of Physicians) a separate College of Paediatrics and Child Health was created in October 1996, and granted a royal charter almost immediately afterwards. Paediatrics, the medical specialty for child health, now has many subspecialties such as paediatric neurology, paediatric orthopaedic surgery and community paediatrics. Specialties have developed for different age groups in childhood, such as neonatal medicine and adolescent medicine. Specialization in nursing has grown along similar lines and health care now encompasses a number of key areas of work such as physiotherapy, speech and language therapy, and play therapy in which special expertise in work with children is firmly established.

The development of areas of special expertise in child health extends to appropriate special facilities such as are found on children's wards, children's intensive care units, and children's facilities in accident and emergency departments. In their totality, these services are regarded as providing the best treatment and environment for relieving children's suffering and restoring them to health. Standards and guidelines have been developed for many of the different aspects of child health care, based upon commonly agreed ideas about the best interests of the child, and taking account of the relevant ethical issues, which may be far from straightforward and are continually evolving. A useful guide for commissioners and providers is given in a publication from Action for Sick Children (Hogg, 1996), and many of the ethical issues are discussed by Campbell (1988) and Kurtz (1996a).

Apart from increasing specialization among the professions working with children, a highly important aspect in the development of practice has been the acknowledgement of the fundamental role played by parents in their children's health and the management of illness, and thereby of the need for professionals to work with parents if services to children are to be effective (De'Ath, 1986). Much of the evidence for this has come from work in the voluntary sector, which has led to far-reaching changes in the way in which health care for children is provided. A prime example is the work of the former National Association for the Welfare of Children in Hospital (NAWCH), which campaigned, among other things, for facilities for parents to stay with their children when they were admitted to hospital (overnight if necessary). Largely through the efforts of NAWCH, the Department of Health produced guidelines covering many aspects of the quality of care for children in hospital (Department of Health, 1991).

The involvement of parents in decisions about their children's care is embodied in the Children Act 1989. This Act and the United Nations Convention on the Rights of the Child have also led to recommendations as well as case law regarding the need to involve children themselves in decisions that affect them (Mitchels and Prince 1992; BMA *et al.*, 1994; British Paediatric Association *et al.*, 1995). For a useful review of children's rights, see Chapter 1 'Children and the law' by Mary Ryan (pp. 7–16). The Department of Health's 1991 guidance states:

> Like all other patients, children have a right for their privacy to be respected and to be treated with tact and understanding. They have an equal right to

information appropriate to their age, understanding and specific circumstances.... Young people should be kept as fully informed as possible about their treatment so as to enable them to exercise their rights. Even where young children do not have the required understanding, they should be provided with as much information as possible and their wishes ascertained and taken into account.

It was not until post-surgery outcomes were shown in a scientific trial to be better in infants who were given complete anaesthesia that the extent of stress and pain suffered by babies who were incompletely anaesthetized was appreciated (Rogers, 1992). Thus scientific evidence is becoming available to reinforce the understanding that the feelings of even the youngest children, and of their parents, contribute to improvement in outcomes of treatment and care (Alderson and Montgomery, 1996). There is further recognition that outcomes such as being able to return to school may be more important for the child and the family than those (such as the consequences of less than rigid adherence to a particular treatment regimen) traditionally held to be important by the health service.

The health care needs of children

Children make up over a quarter of the population. According to the 1991 census, the proportion of children in England and Wales, meaning people under the age of 20, was 27 per cent for males and 24 per cent for females. This is a fall from the proportions in 1841 of 47 and 45 per cent. But in the 150 years since 1841, there has been a threefold increase in total population numbers, so that in 1991 the absolute number of young people aged under 20 was of the order of 13 million (Botting, 1995). The age structure of the minority ethnic groups in the population is younger than that of the population as a whole. These groups comprise not quite 6 per cent of the total population, but about 10 per cent of the child population (10 to 14 years) is non-white. The size of the child population has changed little in more recent years, but, as one would expect, the proportion differs in various parts of the country and between urban and rural situations. In some places, there are higher proportions of the very young and in others, of teenagers.

Children are widely regarded as the healthiest age group; whereas 150 years ago a third of children died before the end of childhood, death rates continue to decline, even over recent years. For males born in 1950, 96.6 per cent survived to the age of one year compared with 99.1 per cent of those born in 1990. Comparative figures for females are 97.4 per cent and 99.3 per cent. Similar improvements are seen at ages 5, 15 and 20. At all ages in childhood there is increased risk of mortality with lower social class, most marked at ages 1 to 4. Boys are consistently at higher risk than girls. Injury and poisoning are the major cause of death for boys aged one and over and for girls aged 5 and over, and accidents are the commonest cause of UK hospital admissions in children aged 5 to 16.

However, the heartening improvements in mortality (compared with previous decades, more children are surviving infancy and childhood to become adults) have diverted attention from the extent of morbidity in childhood and adolescence. Birthweight is a marker of growth *in utero* and is associated with subsequent growth and adult height. It is also a powerful predictor of infant survival and is strongly related to subsequent morbidity. The proportion of all births weighing 3500 g and over (which have the lowest mortality rates) increased during the 1980s, but so did the proportion of babies born alive weighing less than 1500 g. Low birthweight remains a major contributor to mortality in the first weeks of life. Nevertheless, more low-birthweight babies are surviving than previously, with an associated rise in the prevalence of adverse sequelae, which include cerebral palsy and defects of sight and hearing (Botting, 1995; Emsley *et al.*, 1998). Even so, children today are generally taller and healthier than in previous generations.

Very little information is routinely collected about the state of health of the nation's children, except for mortality rates (Department of Health, 1989). The information given in this section is taken largely from a unique recent summary, 'The health of our children', with analyses of data from many different sources including special studies (Botting, 1995). Much of the information that can be used to describe morbidity was collected for other purposes. An example is the prevalence estimated for children requiring special education provision under the 1981 Education Act, which was produced for the report of the Warnock Committee (Department of Education and Science and Welsh Office, 1978). It was reported that 2 per cent of children have a continuing need for special education provision because of severe difficulties with learning. These include children with severe problems related to vision, hearing, speech, physical and neurological function associated with conditions such as cerebral palsy and epilepsy, and to psychological problems. If children with milder functional impairments such as uncomplicated asthma, correctable visual or hearing impairments, and moderate emotional disturbance are included, the prevalence is about 20 per cent. There is some suggestion from the General Household Surveys, carried out regularly by the Office for Population Censuses and Surveys (OPCS), that rates of long-standing illness among children aged 5 to 15 increased during the 1980s. In recent years almost 1 in 5 children were reported as suffering from a long-standing illness, although only about 50 per cent of these had a resulting limitation in activities. Respiratory illness was the major type of health problem, reported by 7 per cent of respondents, and accounts for over half of GP consultations for children aged 0 to 15. The prevalence of severe disability, in a survey carried out in 1985/86, was found to be 3 per cent, with each child identified as disabled having on average 2.7 of the 11 categories of disability, and with behavioural disability the most commonly found overall (in 2 per cent of children) (Bone and Meltzer, 1986).

The only routinely available indicator of mental health in young people is suicide rates. For males aged 15 to 19, these increased by almost 45 per cent between the late 1970s and the late 1980s; comparable rates for teenage girls fell by 23 per cent over the same period. From analysis of a large number of studies from different parts of Europe, there is now good evidence that emotional and behavioural disorders have risen in prevalence over the past 50 years (Rutter and Smith, 1995), and that between 14 and 20 per cent of children will be affected. British studies have found that moderate or severe behaviour problems were present in 7 per cent of inner-city 3-year-olds and that rates of mental health problems rise in adolescence (Maughan in Botting, 1995). The prevalence of anorexia nervosa is around 2 per 1000 in women and girls, with the highest rates (at about 10 per 1000) in middle-class schoolgirls.

The importance for children's health of certain behaviours, in children themselves and in their parents (particularly the mother), is increasingly recognized. Diet, physical activity and smoking are linked to risk of coronary artery disease; diet and smoking again, and exposure to ultraviolet light, are linked to cancer risk; smoking is associated with respiratory illness; and there are significant consequences of alcohol and drug use in the young, and of teenage pregnancy. The health of the mother and her behaviour such as smoking have significant effects on birthweight and on the longer-term health of the child. Awareness has grown of widespread instances of neglect and abuse of children, and the long-lasting, often serious consequences for young people's health have been established. Mental illness in parents is a major risk factor for mental disorder in their children. Similarly, chronic ill health in parents, leading to unemployment and socioeconomic disadvantage, can have serious and long-lasting consequences for children. Children who take on a significant burden of care of a parent are likely to experience many difficulties, including loss of schooling and of peer friendships (Aldridge and Becker, 1995).

Challenges presented by children to the health care system, and by the system to children

Nature of children's health care needs

That chronic illness lasting into adult life is the most prominent feature in the current pattern of ill health in children is a major challenge to the health care system. An important feature is that the long-standing nature of the conditions leads to the development of secondary complications, and these manifestations, as well as others, have to a great extent not been met with previously. In addition, unlike the chief causes of morbidity in former times (infectious diseases), the health problems that affect children today are to a great extent caused not by a single factor, but by a number of factors (Alberman and Peckham, 1986). Cure is rarely possible and often prevention requires multipronged approaches that span new and non-medical fields. In order to tackle these conditions effectively, early detection followed by appropriate intervention is required, and, there-after, close attention to the developmental progress of the child coupled with interventions that keep pace with the emergence of new manifesta-tions of the chronic condition and with the interaction between its manifestations and the other important aspects of the child's life.

Many conditions in childhood are not clearly apparent at the time that the first suspicions are aroused. A well-documented example is mild to moderate cerebral palsy. Even with a more clear-cut example such as hearing defect, recent evidence documents continuing reasons for unacceptable delays in diagnosis and in instituting treatment (National Deaf Children's Society, 1994). In order to support the child and family over periods of uncertainty at the time of making a diagnosis and when the likely outcome may not be certain, the health service needs to provide professional advice that is believed to be expert by the family, and to offer continuing oversight in a manner that is sympathetic, so as to build up a relationship of trust. Often, significant manifestations of a condition are first seen in school or school is where the most serious problems, from the family's point of view, arise. Educational methods may be central in treatment. If the health and education services do not work together, it is more than likely that any treatment offered by either service will not result in the most effective improvement (Kurtz, 1994a).

Organizational response

In spite of major developments in policy and practice, and the publication of detailed guidelines, there remain many barriers to the relationships that need to be developed – with parents, with the child, between professionals within the child health services, and between professionals working in different agencies. First there is good evidence that improvements are needed in the way that information, advice and guidance are given to parents and children, and in the extent to which professionals learn from the families they care for (see p. 109). The result is often that misunderstandings develop between the family and their professional advisers; the child may stop attending for routine appoinmtents; necessary adjustments in management are not made; and timely prevention of secondary sequelae is not offered. There is a great deal to be gained if a child has been looked after by professionals who have come to know that child and his or her problems throughout childhood, particularly when the time comes for adult services to take on the care (Kurtz and Hopkins, 1996). If this has not been the case, the consequences of being, or having fallen, outside the system can be disastrous, resulting, for example, in early severe complications such as blindness in a young person with insulin-dependent diabetes (British Paediatric Association, 1989). The challenges to health services include not only the need for training in talking to young people, but in maintaining expertise and keeping up to date with the rapid advances in medicine, including the emergence of an ever-increasing number of conditions, many of which even child health specialists may see only rarely during their careers.

The planning, funding and organization of child health services do not encourage the flexible arrangements that support continuity in management and ready access between professional staff and families. Owing to modern employment conditions and career considerations, children and families may well meet a large number of professionals over the years. Often, no one professional retains overall responsibility or an updated knowledge and understanding of the issues for care in all domains of a child's life. If opinion and treatment from different specialists are required, this will become an inevitable concern. Difficulties for the family and for optimum management of the child's condition are compounded by the number of different provider trusts in which staff work, by different management structures between professional groups such as paediatricians, community nurses, psychologists and therapists, and by the different agencies that may need to be involved. In the health service, guidelines to integrate care between the primary, secondary and tertiary sectors exist (British Paediatric Association, 1991, 1992; Department of Health, 1991; Verrier Jones and Lissauer, 1995); similarly, for integrated work between social services and health (Home Office *et al.*, 1991) and between education and health services (DfE, 1994). However, although on the ground practitioners may work collaboratively in many instances, these arrangements are often tenuous because they are not supported by strategic agreements between different sectors or by secure funding arrangements. Setting these up is the responsibility of the health commissioner together with local social services and education authorities. There is promise of improvement as a result of mandatory children's services planning, with the guidance that this must be carried out jointly with health services and education (Department of Health *et al.*, 1996). However, there still seems a long way to go before the statutory duties of local authorities and their priorities in resource allocation can be matched harmoniously with those of the health service

(Kurtz, 1994a, 1996b). Agreement about which of children's needs are the greatest and which methods are effective in meeting them are problematic even within the field of medicine, but are fraught with difficulty when considered across different knowledge bases and professional disciplines. There is no shortage of ideas about best practice, but implementing and sustaining them present many difficulties when each health authority may have to negotiate with several local authorities (each with perhaps a different local agenda) in planning services for its resident population, must involve local GPs in strategic planning and must be advised by different professional groups with differing ideas about service development.

Using evidence to guide strategic decision-making has become a major policy initiative (Ham *et al.*, 1995). The basis of health authority funding and rationing decisions rests on what is known about the ability of people with particular problems to benefit from particular provision. However, in the majority of instances, little is known in this respect, or what is known has not been incorporated into the knowledge base currently used in commissioning; further, what is known may be incomplete or of doubtful quality. There remains a huge challenge in improving this fundamentally important evidence base for setting priorities and obtaining adequate resources in many areas of health care. The challenges seem particularly great in the health care of children because, as has been mentioned, many of the problems that they face are new and under-researched. There are particular difficulties in obtaining the evidence that is needed about outcomes throughout the developmental stages of childhood. In adult life, adverse outcomes of chronic conditions are well understood but data relating to the course of illness during childhood are both scant and hard to come by (Johnson, 1997). The evaluation of preventive strategies is similarly fraught with difficulties, mainly because it takes too long for the relevant findings to be gathered, and in the meantime services that can show more immediate benefit are financed. Furthermore, there are greater difficulties in obtaining the views of children than of adults as to the outcomes that for them are the most important (see p. 110).

The move to tailor services according to evidence of benefit and value for money has led to poor funding or the cutting of services for which the demonstration of benefit has, up until now, had inadequate showing; speech therapy and psychotherapy are good examples. Child health surveillance programmes have been streamlined to include only tests for impairment and disablity of proven validity. This means that these routine visits to the doctor and health visitor are no longer an opportunity for parents to raise matters of concern in a casual way and for the professional to give time for this to happen, to get to know children and their families, and to carry out important informal observations. Many suspect that a most valuable component of the programme is thus lost, but this is difficult to prove (Hall, 1996).

National health policy stresses the importance of prevention (Secretary of State, 1992), and in this, health in infants and children is chiefly seen as important in the long-term success of the strategy for improved health in adults. In 1992 some targets were set as indicators of improved health in children; that is, reductions in mortality from accidents, reductions in teenage conceptions and reductions in the number of children smoking. It was acknowledged that achievement of these targets required the efforts of services and of government departments other than the NHS and the Department of Health. Childhood accidents are a prime example of a health issue which has outcomes of considerable importance to the health service, but the challenge is to institute and co-ordinate preventive action in many other services and policy areas, including maternal mental health, education, transport, the environment and product standards (Golding in Alberman and Peckham, 1986). The Labour government Green Paper on Public Health (Secretary of State, 1998) places a major emphasis on working with schools to tackle the causes of poor health during childhood.

In almost all areas, children's own behaviour has significant effects upon their health. As children's own experiences become more valued and as they gain greater autonomy, their behaviour will bring greater challenges to health services. Children now live much less in a separate world from adults with regard to accidents, and risk-taking behaviours such as smoking and drug use, but they place greater reliance on their own views and capabilities than in previous times. There is a new challenge in finding ways to enable ever younger children to understand the consequences for their health and well-being of choices that they can now make for themselves. Studies have shown that health in the traditional sense is not of great concern to young people, and that the majority of those with chronic medical conditions do not consider their health to be poor (Kurtz and Hopkins, 1996). What concerns them is their capacity to function, to find friends, do the things they want to do, get a job, get married, and live independently. They avoid health services if they can and understandably value careers and housing services more highly. However, as teenagers, children with one health problem, such as asthma, show a greater risk, as compared with their peers without problems, of developing further difficulties, especially emotional and behavioural problems. There is still a stigma attached to having an illness, particularly mental illness. The challenge to the health system to find ways to encourage children and young people to make good use of services that can minimize any health problems they may have and not to neglect their health as a resource for living, is obvious.

The challenge of access to health services is particularly great for certain groups of children. These include those whose parents suffer socioeconomic disadvantage, or who are themselves ill, or who do not speak English as a first language, or who are immigrants, or those who, for whatever reason, do not understand the system. They also include children who are looked after by the local authority or who are in residential accommodation such as a boarding special school. Children such as these are known to have particular risks of health problems and to be liable to miss out on routine health and preventive services, as well as to have poor access to special provision even when they are in obvious need. A further group of children who present a challenge in terms of access are those whose helpable problems are not recognized; they include children with depression, who may be ignored while the acting-out child will receive attention.

The impact of advances in health care technology

Advances in knowledge and the technologies for the treatment of disease conditions in children bring challenges to the health services and to children even though they now have improved survival and, in many instances, improved relief from suffering and disability. These advances have meant that many children now live with a disease condition. The progression of these disease conditions, as well as the effects of treatments over the long term, require new kinds of management and have, as a result, become new fields in health care. A good example is the treatment of childhood cancer. Twenty to thirty years ago, cure was contemplated for less than 25 per cent of all children who developed cancer. The overall cure rate for childhood cancer in the UK is now over 60 per cent and for some types more than 90 per cent (Morris-Jones and Craft, 1990, quoted in Kurtz and Tomlinson, 1991). However, long-term follow-up studies have recently shown that many children have significant problems resulting from their successful treatment. These include renal and cardiovascular dysfunction, problems with fertility, secondary tumours, neuropsychological sequelae and social problems. As one in 600 children develops cancer before their fifteenth birthday, by the year 2000 at least one in 1000 young adults will have been cured of cancer as child. In addition to longer-term consequences, during the period of treatment the child's immunity is compromised, leading to greater risk from infections such as measles.

   The new knowledge and techniques that are available to treat and manage many conditions in children have led to the development of super-specialists among child health experts and to special units where the expertise of many professionals, such as nursing, physiotherapy, psychology and medicine, can be brought together in a team and where special equipment can be made available. Although these centres are necessary to provide the highest quality in diagnosis, assessment and treatment, and for further research and the development of knowledge and expertise, they are expensive, and rarely required for more than a small number of children resident in any one health authority. In addition, because only a small number of centres in the country as a whole specialize in any one condition such as cystic fibrosis or congenital heart conditions, each centre is likely to be located at some distance from an individual health authority. This raises significant challenges for health authorities in ensuring standards of care and value for money from the range of specialist services, local and distant, that may be indicated for a particular child. There are further challenges in ensuring the necessary continuity of care over the long term, including the responsibility for maintaining an overview of a number of facets of care such as the child's continuing education and support for the family. Recognition of the complexity that now attends proper care of children with conditions such as cystic fibrosis and childhood leukaemia has led to the publication of guidelines for development of services nationally (Clinical Standards Advisory Group, 1993a, b). The British Paediatric Association published a general review of the present position and future needs entitled 'Tertiary services for children and young people' (Verrier Jones and Lissauer, 1995). Figure 6.1 (taken from this publication) indicates the network of necessary relationships between services and agencies. The challenges to all levels of the NHS are seen here particularly clearly. They include how to maintain and develop the most advanced knowledge and skills in a health care system that relies for the funding of the treatment of children at specialist national or regional centres on decisions and priorities of many different health authorities across the country. National guidance on how specialist centres should work with local secondary care services has been given in the Calman–Hine Report (Department of Health, 1995), focused upon cancer services; and on how a number of health authorities can commission specialist services they each require on a shared basis (National Health Service Management Executive, 1993). The challenges in integrating care from different service elements so that all efforts are reinforced and children are not left to fall between stools are described in the case of child and adolescent mental health by the National Health Service Health Advisory Service (1995).

Within health commissions, further challenges are raised by the choices that have to be made regarding which children to treat and for how long to continue treatment. These choices have to be made as part of setting priorities for the use of resources, and also in balancing the extent of clinical benefit against the costs of treatment, including the cost of suffering, as treatments may themselves be extremely unpleasant or painful. One example is the continuing debate over health service policy regarding the optimum use of expensive neonatal intensive care resources; this centres around the birthweight below which the risk of saving a baby who is seriously damaged is unacceptable (Robertson, 1993). The

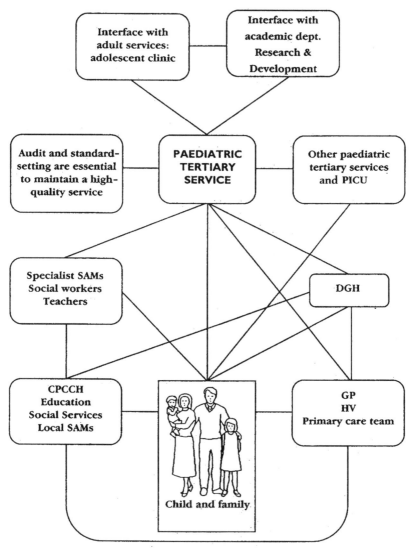

Interfaces for the child with chronic illness receiving specialist paediatric tertiary care. The child and family are central to the process. Considerable skill is required in organization and communication to make proper use of the services available and maximize the benefit to the child.

DGH – district general hospital
HV – health visitor
GP – general practitioner

CPCCH – consultant paediatrician
community child health
SAMs – specialisms allied to medicine

Figure 6.1 Relationships between primary, secondary and tertiary care for children and their families (from Verrier Jones and Lissauer, 1995)

dilemma was highlighted in the following statement in a report of the Royal College of Physicians on the medical care of the newborn in England and Wales (1988, p. iv): 'Finally ... there is the question of whether we can better afford the economic cost of providing appropriate standards of care for ill new-born babies, or the moral cost of failing to do so.'

Health authorities seek to control expenditure by setting criteria by which they will fund their providers. Serious conflict may arise in this respect between the health authority and provider clinicians, who may want to make the decision to treat in individual cases in the light of their own professional judgement. Clinicians may, of course, have differences of opinion from parents, who may then seek treatment elsewhere. These issues were raised by the case of 'Child B', a 10-year-old girl with myeloid leukaemia, for whom funding for a further course of treatment was turned down by her district health authority, on the clinical grounds that the chances of success, were, it was felt, too low and the suffering caused by the treatment unacceptably great. 'B's' father did not accept this, and appealed to the High Court to overturn the district health authority's decision. The costs in terms of pain and suffering to 'B' were felt by her father and stepmother to be bearable in the best interests of her chance of survival. However, because they wished to protect her 'from knowledge about her risk of dying', 'B' herself was never given the opportunity to give fully informed consent, let alone to refuse treatment, and so no one knew what her best interests truly were. One measure of effectiveness (cure or remission) was given very much greater emphasis than the quality-of-life dimension; this is usually the case in making decisions on the provision of services, for an individual and for a population. Measurement of quality of life requires the views of the person with the condition under question, and, as yet, we have very little experience in ascertaining these views in children (Kurtz, 1996a).

Rapidly growing technologies that allow antenatal detection of conditions such as Down's syndrome or cystic fibrosis lead to challenges of a different nature. Ethical dilemmas arise which are constantly shifting, chiefly at the interface between the parents' understanding of the risks and their views about whether or not to continue with the pregnancy and to handle a possible lifetime of caring for a disabled child, and the capacity of the clinical services to support the family's decisions. There is a further interface between what health service providers offer in the way of testing, counselling and support, and whether there is health authority policy and funding for the relevant services. There is considerable variation between authorities, for example, in policies for testing for Down's syndrome in pregnancy. The variation is linked to argument about the extent to which different tests accurately predict whether the baby is or is not affected (Wyllie *et al.*, 1997). Few authorities in Britain have faced the challenge of developing policy regarding the funding of lifelong care of a disabled and handicapped person born to parents who had had antenatal knowledge that their child would be so affected. Agonizing decisions about the use of scarce resources may be made by individual clinicians in deciding whether to treat disease conditions in smokers who will not give up smoking. The risk that a young person will not benefit from treatment of a behaviour disorder may be similarly high if, for example, they cannot overcome serious drug misuse.

The major new developments that have been made in neonatal screening for inherited disorders create a significant dilemma for the National Health Service (Bartlett *et al.*, 1997). The effective detection of an increased number of infants with inherited disease, most of whom are treatable, will place an additional burden on clinical services. However, early detection and treatment of these infants should result in savings to society in that lifelong disability is avoided. Furthermore, even if the prognosis is poor (as it is for some of the rarer conditions) effective screening will at the very least provide parents with genetic advice at an early stage of their reproductive lives. Bartlett and her colleagues conclude that this does not mean that there will be savings to the health service (most probably the reverse) and thus in determining how to spend its limited budget, the NHS has a vested interest in promoting policies that do not result in further financial burdens.

Government policy designed to give women more control over what happens during pregnancy and labour has been implemented because of women's concerns that technology seemed to be taking over childbirth (Department of Health, 1993). The increased use of technology in pregnancy and labour has, however, led to major reductions in the risks to the baby, and therefore in implementing this policy the question has been raised of possible conflict between the safety of the baby and the exercise of the mother's choice.

Concepts of childhood

Ideas about childhood and perceptions of children have changed enormously even in the past 20 years. As the Court Committee (Department of Health and Social Security *et al.*, 1976) recognized:

> In the last two or three generations we have come to realise their needs as being different from those of adults. At one time children were dressed in adult clothes scaled down to size, which seemed to reflect an attitude that they were in a sense retarded adults. Childhood was thought of as an inadequate and incomplete form of the adult state. By contrast we have become increasingly aware of childhood as a separate state, as a period of human experience in its

own right. And more important still, we have come to realise the extent to which experience in childhood determines adult outcome. (p. 2)

A significant challenge is presented by the requirement, under the Children Act 1989 and in accordance with the UN Convention on the Rights of the Child, to involve children in decisions that affect them. In health care, this should extend to their involvement in the overall planning and evaluation of service provision (in setting priorities and standards of quality) and in outcome measurement; and to having their wishes taken into account with regard to individual treatment and care. Decision-making processes about individual children cannot be deemed ethical if the child is not properly included (see the case of 'Child B', p. 107). In regard to the introduction of anaesthesia for infant surgery, we have seen how, apart from humanitarian considerations, outcomes of treatment may be improved when children's feelings are taken into account. There is recognition that many professionals find it difficult not only to talk directly to children about health-related topics but also to believe in the ability of children to understand such matters and to exercise reasonable judgement on their own account. Even more difficult for many professionals is the capacity to listen to children and to learn from what they have to say about themselves. However, thoughtful guidelines based on careful research are now available for all who work with children, including very young children (Alderson and Montgomery, 1996). An interesting project, Youth Voice, has been started by the Trust for the Study of Adolescence to enable young people to communicate their ideas and concerns to professionals and to contribute to the training of adults who have direct and regular contact with young people (Neary, 1997).

For the most part, and traditionally, parents make the decisions regarding their children's health care, and professionals talk almost exclusively to parents. Guidelines are now available for situations with particular sensitivities and difficulties such as may arise in communicating with families whose first language is not English or who are from non-mainstream cultural and religious backgrounds, and in communicating details of very serious disease conditions to all families (Lingam and Newton, 1996). But a challenge to all who work in the health services is that of arriving at decisions primarily for the child's benefit when the parents may be the sole spokespersons. A body of case law has been built up to guide professionals, based upon the Gillick ruling on confidentiality for under-16-year-olds in health care consultation (Mitchels and Prince, 1992) and on consent to treatment and the withholding of treatment (Alderson, 1993b; Elton *et al.*, 1995; Royal College of Paediatrics and Child Health, 1997). But the lives of children may be vulnerable in the extreme, caught between the need to agree decisions between parents, clinicians and funders of health services. This is illustrated in two types of situation. In a recent decision (*Re T*, 24 October 1996), the Court of Appeal ruled that it was not in the best interests of an 18-month-old boy to undergo a potentially life-saving liver transplant against the wishes of his parents, even though his doctors agreed that without the transplant, the boy would die in less than a year and that with it, his prognosis for long-term recovery would be very good (Frantz, 1997). A second type is where children are subjected to testing for genetic conditions (Kurtz, 1998). Situations of acute conflict may arise in making decisions about whether or not to terminate a pregnancy where the baby is thought to be affected by a congenital defect. It is the commonly held view that the mother has the right to make the decision about the survival of the unborn child. For a child born with certain conditions, such as cystic fibrosis, where progress in gene therapy has been made, it is now likely that he or she will be enabled to live a normal life span. In this situation, has the mother the right to override her unborn child's right to live? (Kurtz, 1994b)

Involving children in larger planning decisions about health care is even more problematic. Mechanisms hardly exist for consulting with young people as a body, let alone on a regular or routine basis and with reliable representation of comprehensive viewpoints. However, mention must be made of Article 12, a group of young people seeking to promote opportunities (such as in planning health care) for the views of children to be taken into account. Article 12 was launched in November 1996, supported by the Children's Rights Development Unit, and is located at the National Children's Bureau. Children under voting age are not part of the nation's democratic processes. In the National Health Service in Britain, children do not have independent rights to services in that they cannot vote under the age of 18 years, and according to the Children Act 1989, the definition of a child is a person under this age. Children do not have citizens' rights. Thus the 1991 Patient's Charter restates from the NHS Act of 1946 that:

> Every citizen has the right
> 1. to receive health care on the basis of clinical need, regardless of ability to pay; and
> 2. to be given a clear explanation of any treatment proposed, including any risks and any alternatives, before you decide whether you will agree to treatment.

Guidelines on services for children and young people under the Patient's Charter were produced in April 1996. These are addressed throughout to parents with respect to their children, and children's rights to health care are limited to the right to be registered with a general practitioner. Statute in regard to children's needs relies on the Children Act 1989, which is less than satisfactory in relation to health services. The Act seeks primarily to support parents in their duty to care for their children, and requires local authorities (but not health authorities independently) to make services available when a child can be defined as 'in need'. In implementing the Act, criteria for the designation of a 'child in need' have been found to vary between authorities, and a health authority must comply with the request for help from a local authority provided only that the request is compatible with its own statutory and other duties and does not unduly prejudice the discharge of its function (Section 27).

Following its ratification of the United Nations Convention on the Rights of the Child, the UK government was required to report, after a three-year period, on how its policies and practice fit in with the principles of the Convention. When the UN Committee commented on the UK report, it noted in particular that the principle of the best interests of the child appears not to be reflected in legislation and regulations in such areas as health, education and social security which have a bearing on the respect for the rights of the child. Covering a whole range of concerns, the committee identified that in the UK negative or at least 'not positive' attitudes to children are widespread and that their best interests are pursued, or perhaps merely safeguarded, in ways that are neither comprehensive nor coherent but indeed often conflicting.

National expenditure on children's health services is disproportionately low in relation to the proportion of children in the population: hospital and community health services' gross current expenditure on the age group 0 to 15 years (19 per cent of the total population) is 13.2 per cent of that for all ages, excluding expenditure on births, and 18.3 per cent if births expenditure is included (1995/96 estimate, Department of Health, 1998). Systems of resource allocation in the NHS have relied largely on indicators of need for an illness service. More money is made available to areas where mortality rates are higher, and to services that treat the chief causes of death (Carr-Hill *et al.*, 1994). In this respect, children, with low overall mortality rates, appear to merit low funding. Recently, even, there has been evidence of inadequate resources such that only half the children identified as requiring intensive care receive it in paediatric intensive care units (British Paediatric Association, 1993).

Further challenges arise when young people's views, best interests or behaviours run seriously counter to those of powerful and/or well-informed policy-makers. The views of particular groups need to be reconciled, such as those who have a disability or those from particular religious backgrounds. The dilemmas are highlighted by guidance on male circumcision of newborn infants on demand by parents, issued by the General Medical Council in September 1997. It was forced to act after receiving complaints about standards of care and letters questioning the ethics of the practice. The guidance says that doctors performing the operation must be skilled in it, keep up to date with developments and discuss the issues carefully with parents. However, it does not answer the ethical question of whether it is right to perform the operation for religious or cosmetic reasons (report by Jeremy Laurance, Health Editor of *The Independent*, 22 September 1997). An estimated one in five men in the UK is circumcised. Critics argue that where there is no medical justification for the procedure it amounts to an assault. Professor Sir Cyril Chantler (Chairman of the General Medical Council's standards committee) had stated that male circumcision was legal and the question of whether it was ethical had to be decided by society, not doctors. If doctors did not carry out the procedure, parents would be driven to back-street clinics. Some 'strong views' had been expressed to the General Medical Council by religious organizations, professional and patient groups, and children's organizations. Many had recognized the difficulty of balancing the rights of the child with the rights of individuals to practise their religion. However, experts writing in the *British Medical Journal* question the legality of the procedure, with concerns about whether, when these children grow up, they may ask why it was done.

Conclusion

In health care, children generally rely on the knowledge, skills and goodwill of others, usually their parents and also doctors, nurses and many more; all of them can act as advocates for the best interests of the child. A major challenge follows the recognition that gains in health can be of many kinds and that we need the expertise of all these people, and of children themselves, to identify and maximize the benefit. The challenge to the state is to find ways to enable the development throughout society of a more positive vision of the importance of promoting the health of children and of caring for them in ill health, based on coherent and comprehensive views of what our society wants its children to be and of what roles children themselves want to play in society.

Health care policy for children cannot be separated from policy for other age groups and in other areas of life. Depending upon the importance given by society to the well-being of its young, a further challenge must be for government departments to set up mechanisms to accurately monitor the impact on children of policies made in every area.

The health care system itself faces a number of serious challenges. The first is to develop organizational and management structures to overcome the fragmentation that currently exists in the way health problems are dealt with. This entails professions and agencies together facing challenges regarding accountability for the ways in which their resources are spent and what kinds of work they do. There is no question that assumptions about the purpose of health services based on traditional roles need to be challenged; and along with this, traditional ideas about what it means to do the job of a doctor or a nurse. The challenge for professionals is to adapt in order to meet the changing needs of children rather than to stand still for reasons or needs of their own. But there is also sense in treading cautiously, in order to have time to bring thought and careful attention to the increasingly complex issues that face those who plan and practise health care. Linked to this is the daunting challenge of ensuring that the best new knowledge and skills are acquired, disseminated and utilized in all parts of the system. The structural changes that will be set up in response to the NHS White Paper (Department of Health, 1997) emphasize co-operation as opposed to competition between service providers, and may yet open the door to more effective learning and communication.

Most difficult of all, the health care system must move away from measuring its success in children's health in terms of death rates, or the number of FCEs (finished consultant episodes) achieved in any one year by a department. This requires an even closer relationship between those who deliver the services (clinicians and managers) and those who use them, with a more sensitive and sensible understanding of when the services are doing well, and with more realistic expectations on all sides. There is further challenge in achieving greater equity in provision, and in finding ways to help children who are particularly vulnerable, who still tend to be neglected. Central to the success of our health care system must be a major positive contribution to improvements in the well-being of children and to their capacity to enjoy their lives to the full.

References

Alberman, E.D. and Peckham, C.S. (eds) (1986) Childhood epidemiology. *British Medical Bulletin*, 42 (2), 117–219.

Alderson, P. (1993a) *Children's Consent to Surgery*. Buckingham: Open University Press.

Alderson, P. (ed.) (1993b) Young people, psychiatric treatment and consent. London: Social Security Research Unit.

Alderson, P. and Montgomery, J. (1996) *Health Care Choices: Making Decisions with Children*. London: Institute for Public Policy Research.

Aldridge, J. and Becker, S. (1995) Children who care. In B. Franklin (ed.), *The Handbook of Children's Rights*. London: Routledge.

Audit Commission (1994) Seen but not heard: co-ordinating community child health and social services for children in need. London: HMSO.

Bartlett, K., Eaton, S.J. and Pourfarzam, M. (1997) New developments in neonatal screening. *Archives of Disease in Childhood*, 77, F151–F154.

BMA, GMSC, HEA, Brook Advisory Centres, FPA and RCGP (1994) Confidentiality and people under sixteen – joint guidance. London.

Bone, M. and Meltzer, H. (1986) The prevalence of disability among children. OPCS. London: HMSO.

Botting, B. (ed.) (1995) The health of our children: the Registrar's decennial supplement for England and Wales. Series DS no. 11; OPCS. London: HMSO.

British Paediatric Association (1989) Report of a working party into the organisation of services for children with diabetes in the United Kingdom. London: BPA.

British Paediatric Association. (1991) Towards a combined child health service. London: BPA.

British Paediatric Association (1992) Management models in established combined or integrated child health services. London: BPA.

British Paediatric Association (1993) The care of critically ill children: report of a multi-disciplinary working party on intensive care. London: BPA.

British Paediatric Association, Children's Rights Development Unit, Royal College of Nursing and the International Child Health Group (1995) Child health rights: implementing the UN Convention on the Rights of the Child within the National Health Service – a practitioner's guide. London.

Butler, J.R. (1989) Child health surveillance in primary care: a critical review. London: HMSO.

Campbell, A.G.M. (1988) Ethical issues in child health and disease. In J. Forfar (ed.), *Child Health in a Changing Society*. London: British Paediatric Association.

Carr-Hill, R., Sheldon, T., Smith, P., Martin, S., Peacock, S. and Hardman, G. (1994) Allocating resources to health authorities: development of methods for small area analysis and use of inpatient services. *British Medical Journal*, 309, 1046–9.

Clinical Standards Advisory Group (1993a) Childhood leukaemia: access to and availability of specialist services. London: HMSO.

Clinical Standards Advisory Group (1993b) Specialist Services for cystic fibrosis. London: HMSO.

De'Ath, E. (ed.) (1986). Developing a partnership with parents in the child health services. Partnership paper 8. London: National Children's Bureau.

Department of Education and Science and Welsh Office (1978) Special Educational Needs: Report of the Committee of Inquiry into the Education of Handicapped Children and Young People (Chairperson: Mrs Mary Warnock). London: HMSO.

Department for Education and Welsh Office (1994) Code of practice on the identification and assessment of special educational needs. London: HMSO.

Department of Health (1989) Health of the population: children. In *On the State of the Public Health for the Year 1988*, pp. 61–2. London: HMSO.

Department of Health (1991) Welfare of children and young people in hospital. London: HMSO.

Department of Health (1993) Changing childbirth: report of the Expert Maternity Group (Chairperson: Baroness Cumberlege). London: HMSO.

Department of Health (1995) A policy framework for commissioning cancer services 1995: report of an expert advisory group (Calman-Hine Report). London: DoH.

Department of Health (1997) The new NHS: modern, dependable. London: DoH.

Department of Health (1998) Departmental report: The Government's Expenditure Plans, 1998–1999. London: The Stationery Office.

Department of Health, Department for Education and NHS Executive (1996) *Children's Services Planning Amendment Order under Section 17(4) of the Children Act 1989.*

Department of Health and Social Security, Department of Education and Science and Welsh Office, (1976) Fit for the future: report of the Committee on Child Health Services (Chairperson: Professor Donald Court), vol. I. London: HMSO.

Elton, A., Honig, P., Bentovim, A. and Simons, J. (1995) Withholding consent to lifesaving treatment: three cases. *British Medical Journal*, **310**, 373–7.

Emsley, H.C.A., Wardle, S.P., Sims, D.G., Chiswick, M.L. and D'Souza, S.W. (1998) Increased survival and deteriorating outcome in 23 to 25 week old gestation infants, 1990–4 compared with 1984–9. *Archives of Disease in Childhood*, **78** (2), F99–F104.

Forfar, J. (ed.) (1988) *Child Health in a Changing Society*. London: British Paediatric Association.

Frantz, C. (1997) A matter of life and death: is a transplant in the best interests of a child? *CHILDRIGHT* January/February, no. 133, 4–5.

Hall, D. (ed.) (1996) *Health for All Children*, 3rd edition. Oxford: Oxford University Press.

Ham, C., Hunter, D.J. and Robinson, R. (1995) Evidence based policymaking. *British Medical Journal*, **310**, 71–2.

Hogg, C. (1996) Health services for children and young people: a guide for commissioners and providers. London: Action for Sick Children.

Home Office, Department of Health, Department of Education and Science and Welsh Office (1991) Working together under the Children Act 1989. London: HMSO.

Johnson, A. (1997) Follow up studies: a case for a standard minimum data set. *Archives of Disease in Childhood*, **76**, F61–F63.

Kurtz, Z. (1994a) Relationships between the health service and local authorities. In: Special child: special needs. Report of a working party on services for children with disabilities (Chairperson: Rita String-fellow). London: Association of Metropolitan Authorities.

Kurtz, Z. (1994b) Children's rights and health care. *Children & Society*, 8 (2), 114–31.

Kurtz, Z. (1996a) Do children's and young people's rights to health care in the UK ensure their best interests? In A. Macfarlane (ed.), *Adolescent Medicine*. London: Royal College of Physicians of London.

Kurtz, Z. (1996b) Treating children well: a guide to using the evidence base in commissioning and managing services for the mental health of children and young people. London: Mental Health Foundation.

Kurtz, Z. (1998) Appropriate paternalism and the best interests of the child. In A. Clarke (ed.), *The Genetic Testing of Children*. Oxford: BIOS Scientific Publishers.

Kurtz, Z. and Hopkins, A. (1996) *The Transition of Young People with Chronic Medical Conditions from Paediatric to Adult Services*. London: Royal College of Physicians.

Kurtz, Z. and Tomlinson, J. (1991) How do we value our children today? As reflected by children's health, health care and policy? *Children & Society*, 5 (3), 207–24.

Lindstrom, B. and Spencer, N. (eds) (1995) *Social Paediatrics*. Oxford: Oxford University Press.

Lingam, S. and Newton, R. (1996) Right from the start: the way parents are told that their child has a disability. London: British Paediatric Association Standing Committee on Paediatric Practice Guidelines (PPG/96/02).

Mitchels, B. and Prince, A. (1992) *The Children Act and Medical Practice*. Bristol: Jordan.

National Children's Bureau (1987) Investing in the future: child health ten years after the Court Report. A report of the Policy and Practice Review Group (Chairperson: Professor Philip Graham). London: NCB.

National Deaf Children's Society (UK) (1994) Quality standards in paediatric audiology: guidelines for the early identification of hearing impairment. London: NDCS.

National Health Service Health Advisory Service (1995) Together we stand: thematic review on the commissioning, role and management of child and adolescent mental health services. London: HMSO.

National Health Service Management Executive (1992) Child health surveillance: a recommended core programme. HSG (92) 19. London: Department of Health. Also Welsh Office, Welsh Health Circular 92 (54).

National Health Service Management Executive (1993) Contracting for specialised services: executive letter (93) 68. London: Department of Health.

Neary, S. (1997) A voice for young people. *Young Minds Magazine*, 30 (July), 10.

Qvortrup, J. (ed.) (1993) Childhood as a social phenomenon: lessons from an international project. Report of a Conference in Billund, Denmark, in September 1992. The European Centre for Social Welfare Policy and Research and the Sydjysk Universitetscenter, Vienna.

Robertson, N.R.C. (1993) Should we look after babies less than 800 grams? *Archives of Disease in Childhood*, **68** (3), 326–9.

Rogers, M.C. (1992) Pain relief in infants and children. *New England Journal of Medicine*, **326**, 55–6.

Royal College of General Practitioners (1982) Healthier children: thinking prevention. Report from General Practice, No. 22. London: RCGP.

Royal College of Paediatrics and Child Health (1997) Withholding or withdrawing life saving treatment in children: a framework for practice. London: RCPCH.

Royal College of Physicians (1988) Medical care of the newborn in England and Wales. Report of an RCP working party. London: RCP.

Rutter, M.T. and Smith, D.J. (1995) *Psychosocial Disorders in Young People*. Chichester: John Wiley on behalf of Academia Europaea.

Secretary of State for Health (1992) The health of the nation: a strategy for England and Wales. London: HMSO.

Secretary of State for Health (1998) *Our Healthier Nation: A Contract for Health*. Consultation paper. London: HMSO.

United Nations Committee on the Rights of the Child (1995) Consideration of reports submitted by States parties under Article 14 of the Convention at the eighth session.

Verrier Jones, K. and Lissauer, T.J. (1995) Tertiary services for children and young people: a guide for the purchase, provision and planning of specialist services for sick children. London: Royal College of Paediatrics and Child Health.

Wyllie, J.P., Madar, R.J., Wright, M., Burn, J. and Wren, C. (1997) Strategies for antenatal detection of Down's syndrome. *Archives of Disease in Childhood*, **76** (1), F26–F30.

7

Social services provision for children and young people: answer or problem?

Jane Tunstill

Are social services part of the *answer* or are they part of the *problem*? The best-known exponent of the iatrogenic analysis of professional activity is probably Ivan Illich (1975), but this question is as crucial to an analysis of social services as it is to health provision. In the context of social services for children it can probably be framed even more specifically as '*Do they prevent more harm than they cause?*'

This question obliges the questioner both to acknowledge the perennial ideological debates around the nature of the relationship between child, family and state, and to raise the spectre of intended *and* unintended outcomes of policy and practice. To complicate the issue even further, any calculation of the benefits and harmful outcomes of social services has to take simultaneous account of the role and function of other areas of policy and provision. Indeed, in many cases the coexistence of social services and other provision results in disjointed and counter-productive policies, such as the current ill fit between welfare-to-work initiatives and campaigns for improved parenting, and between the impact of the Education Reform Act 1988 on school exclusion rates and the scope of family support objectives in the Children Act 1989.

In order to explore the specific potential of social services to facilitate positive outcomes for children and young people, I intend in this chapter to briefly review the history of personal social services in respect of children and families; to map and describe the current configuration of its roles; and to identify and explain the main problems as they are currently perceived.

History and origins of personal social services

If, technically, personal social services provision for children and young people can be said to have its roots in the Seebohm Report (July 1968) more accurately it has emerged over centuries, in the course of what

Heywood (1978) has called the growth of state obligation towards the child.

Some authors (e.g. Hendrick, 1997; James and Prout, 1990) argue that our particular version of received wisdom about the past poses the first challenge to assessing personal social services outcomes for children in the here and now, because of the elusive nature of historical authority and validation. The sphere of social policy as a whole is, as Hendrick (a child care historian) explains, distinguished from other areas of historical inquiry, such as economic, demographic or diplomatic, by the absence of distinctive sources. This has meant that historians have relied heavily on parliamentary papers, national and local government reports, the publications of professional associations and the case and minute books of philanthropic societies, such as the National Society for the Prevention of Cruelty to Children (NSPCC), as well as local authority material on education, health and social welfare. In all of these, to paraphrase Hendrick, lurks the danger of an inevitably circular and biased account because it has been compiled by the predominantly adult middle-class successors of the middle-class adults who designed the systems in the first place. The influence of a socially constructed position has recently gained importance, but I want to argue here that our understanding of outcomes for children *can* still be appropriately located in a traditional theoretical social policy tradition. One of the strengths of such a framework is (precisely) a concern with power inequalities such as class, age and gender, and of course there is no doubt that such phenomena have always shaped the design of policy as well as its subsequent evaluation. Octavia Hill, Lady Allen of Hurtwood, Jane Rowe and Judge Elizabeth Butler-Sloss share more than a common pattern of chromosomes.

However, historiography apart, the second and probably most important complicating factor in reaching a clear view of what social services do to or for children now is the fact that personal social services, like their predecessors, occupy the contested ground between universalism and selectivity. As I have argued elsewhere (Tunstill, 1997) the last 50 years of statutory child care policy and practice can best be understood as the product of the relationship between two significant and interrelated social processes: the beginning of a universal state welfare system and the professionalization of social work. It was the exclusion of social services departments, and very clearly social *work*, from the boundaries of universalism which has had particular implications for child care work, most obviously those aspects of the work which concern children in their own environment, whether family, school or community.

For several centuries, as has been copiously documented, British social policy, inasmuch as it existed, was synonymous with the Poor Law; from the Elizabethan Relief Act of 1601, provision for children mirrored the horrors and advances of the times. For example, as Holman (1998) records, the system could even be said to possess a preventative element in the years immediately preceding the Victorian era. In some parts of the country it was the practice to dispense out-relief to pauper families, the effect of which was to allow them to stay together in their own homes. At the same time, (as Holman also argues), the legacy of the Poor Law ideologies of *less eligibility* and *deterrence* can still be identified in policies for children and their families. However, as Cunningham (1995) among others records, the 1870s witnessed the start of a gradual shift from mere containment and subsistence to ideas of child rescue and reformation, and by way of the notion of the 'Fresh Start' to a far more complex notion and practice of welfare. Ironically it was the emergence of new and, in theory, more enlightened approaches to dealing with children that resulted in compulsory boarding out or fostering in the nineteenth century, during which process some children were cruelly treated or exploited as servants. The most extreme example of the Fresh Start approach was the compulsory emigration of children overseas, which did not end until well into the twentieth century. However, in the context of services for children, the oft-quoted idea that the Poor (or for that matter any other) Law carries the seeds of its own decay has been rivalled in status as an all-purpose policy metaphor by the phenomenon of the 'pendulum swing'. Perhaps this pendulum started to swing seriously in July 1948 when the Children Act was passed with the expressed hope of Lady Allen (a key protagonist) that it should bring to an end 'repressive conditions that are generations out of date', along with the 'chilly stigma of charity'.

The legacy of the past

While the 1948 Children Act, which officially repealed the Poor Law in respect of children, has never been viewed as one of the more exciting Acts within the post-war welfare reforms, it set the context for the subsequent development of provision. It did this in three main ways. First, it rationalized the existing varying and inconsistent standards by means of 'simplification and unification of the administrative machinery' (Packman, 1975), giving regulatory oversight to the Home Office. Its second major legacy was its focus on the relationship between the child and her or his family. In a sense the prescriptive characteristics of the specific relationship espoused by the 1948 Act matter less than the status it accorded to the child–family relationship. Third, and closely associated with this pro-family feature of the Act's intentions, was its status *vis-à-vis* the other more substantial building-blocks of the welfare state:

> If its meaning is to be fully appreciated it has to be seen in relation to the post-war welfare statutes regarded as underpinning the Welfare State: the Family

Allowances Act, 1945, the National Health Service Act (NHS), 1946, and the National Assistance Act 1948. (Hendrick, 1997)

Hendrick sees the main significance of this constellation of social policy laws as rendering the deprived child and the failing parents as an interrelated whole, with the objective of the child care service as being the restoration of the child to the family. However, it could be argued that the very failure of those 1940 reforms to embody policies which would have strengthened family life, such as social security and housing, has bedevilled provision for children and young people, and has led directly to the stigma and social exclusion currently associated with those children and families whose needs are not met by broadly universal, though limited, provision.

To summarize, then, over the decades three key themes – what Hill would call the 'organisational tradition' (1997), Hendrick, the 'familiarisation of childhood' (1997) and I have termed the 'uneasy relationship with universal provision,' – have continued to dominate the course of child care policy and practice by imposing the boundaries of the three key battlefields on which debate has subsequently taken place.

To understand the recent outcomes of social services intervention, or its lack, the next section outlines the current configuration of the roles and responsibilities of personal social services for children and families.

Child and family: the roles and responsibilities of personal social services

As other writers in this volume (in particular Cannan and Newell) demonstrate, the features of English child care policy increasingly need to be set in a broader international, and particularly European, context. This is not to say there is necessarily a comfortable fit between the principles enshrined in, for example, the UN Convention on the Rights of the Child (ratified by the UK in 1991) and the dominant direction of British policy. However, a broader context helps to illuminate the debate about the relationship between rights which derive from the status of *adult* as opposed to the status of *child*, as well as underlining the complexity of the following question : when is the state entitled to intervene in the private lives of families in order to protect children? 'Essential to our understanding of modern childhood, particularly in the UK, is the diminution in parental, particularly paternal, rights over children and growth in the importance of parental duties, obligations and responsibilities towards children' (Brannen and O'Brien, 1996, p. 3).

Fox Harding (1991, 1996) has identified four key elements within this question. When is the state to intervene? How is the state to know and recognize poor-quality child care? What, if any, is the weight to be accorded to the adverse personal or structural circumstances of parents? Is the action the state takes in cases of improper care always helpful?

Millar and Warman (1996) address the same issues from a European perspective. They argue that the key determinant of family policy responses is the way in which governments define family obligations. Obligations between family and state have to be understood at three levels attitude, behaviour and policy. 'The first level is what people believe is right in a given situation. The second is what they actually do when faced with choices; and the third is what the law tells them to do.' (p. 7)

Hardiker *et al.* (1991) explore the parameters of state intervention and in particular distinguish between four levels of intervention: preventing problems from arising (this is probably *not* provided by social services); responding to early stresses and preventing them from getting worse; combating serious problems; and remedial action for those whom the state has taken over. This typology is in many ways similar to the earlier conceptual work done by Parker (1980) which emphasized the notion of a continuum along which it was possible to locate both child protection work and preventive work. Preventive work is aimed at preventing a range of negative outcomes (including the need for such crisis oriented/ protection activity) from arising in the first place. Hardiker *et al.*, believe that children and family social work should focus intervention at the point where it can prevent problems and avoid more intrusive interventions later on. They also emphasize the idea that prevention and protection should be inseparable goals and point to the way that in England and Wales this importance is acknowledged by the Children Act 1989.

Indeed, the Children Act 1989 is the focus of a range of professional aspirations and moral expectations in respect of the relationship between children, family and the state, and its 108 sections provide a clear illustration of the way in which that perennial power struggle between child, family and state has most recently been resolved. Its main provisions are outlined in the next section.

Children Act 1989

The passing of the Children Act 1989 should in theory have greatly simplified the delivery, not to say the study, of personal social services provision for children and young people. Certainly the rhetoric which accompanied its passing was impressive. The Lord Chancellor, Lord Mackay of Clashfern, opened the debate in the House of Lords on the second reading of the Bill with the following words:

> The Bill in my view represents the most comprehensive and far-reaching reform of child care law which has come before Parliament in living memory. It brings

together the public and private law concerning the care, protection and upbringing of children and the provision of services to them and their families.

The Act has an unusually explicit and apparently rational history in that it was preceded by a review of child care law and underpinned by a set of empirical studies commissioned by the Department of Health (Department of Health and Social Security, 1985a, b). Other, less easily quantifiable recorded events, in particular the plethora of child care inquiries, and specifically the Cleveland Inquiry, have also been widely acknowledged to have had a major influence on the aims, objectives and overall philosophy of the Act (Parton, 1991).

The innovations it introduced include, as Lord Mackay emphasized, the fact that it brought together, for the first time, public and private law in respect of children and families, and that the principles that underpin it have been spelled out in an Introduction to the Act (Department of Health, 1990a) and expanded in an extensive published body of Guidance and Regulations (Department of Health, 1990b).

The overarching aims of the Children Act 1989 fall into three main areas, summarized by Aldgate *et al.* (1998). Its first aim is to promote and safeguard the welfare of children whether living with their families or elsewhere. The paramountcy of a child development perspective underlines the fact that children develop best where they have stable adult carers, positive praise and continuity of living circumstances, and also explains the importance of continuity of education, language, race and culture for children in care.

The second aim is to define and promote the concept of parental responsibility. This is defined in the Act as follows:

the collection of duties, rights and authority which a parent has in respect of his child. That choice of words emphasises that the duty to care for the child and to raise him to moral, physical and emotional health is the fundamental task of parenthood and the only justification for the authority it confers.

The state seeks to balance the potential tension between intrusion into family privacy and the protection of children from harm by providing a range of possible outcomes of court cases, preferably in the absence of orders, to underline the principle that families should and indeed can act responsibly towards their children.

The third aim is to define the framework of the legal and organizational responses necessary to achieve the most helpful decisions in court cases and the provision of services best suited to promote the welfare of children in need. This aim requires an inter-agency as well as a social services response and its implementation calls for strategic planning to implement corporate services, as well as an inspection and regulation service to ensure control.

Organizational issues

The formal legal requirements codified in individual pieces of legislation such as the Children Act 1989 are of course vulnerable to qualification, change and modification by the organizational context in which they are implemented. The Children Act is no different from any other.

It might be thought that the debates about organizational characteristics pose the least complex area within any analysis of personal social services provision for children today, but this is not necessarily so. It is impossible to understand the organizational context without addressing the two dimensions cited by Stevenson (1997): the location of child care services within the framework of *local government*; and the effects of the *expansion and managerialism of such services*. This distribution of power between central and local government is especially significant. There is a convincing case to be made for both central government control and local autonomy, but many would argue that the struggle for supremacy over the last 50 years has been to the detriment of services for children at local authority level. Whereas the 1948 Children's Departments were placed firmly under the supervision of the Home Office, and in particular the Child Care Inspectorate, post-1972 social services departments have been the responsibility of the Department of Health and the Social Services Inspectorate. The subsequent problems have been explained in a variety of ways: the loss of specialist skills; the turnover of staff and pressure of work (Holman, 1988) the economic downturn of the 1970s and 1980s, which increased need and reduced collective provision to meet it (Wilding, 1992), and the fact that 'the personal social services were to be caught up in a debate about what may be described as the ideology of welfare. What should the state provide and how?' (Stevenson, 1997, p. 12).

However, the fact remains that organizational explanations cover at least some of the most obvious problems which have recently come to prominence in respect of children and social services departments, including inter-agency cooperation and the adequacy of arrangements for the inspection and regulation of residential care.

This brief overview of current legislative and policy aspirations underlines the enduring nature of the perennial tensions within child care policy. It has been identified by a number of authors (including McGowan, 1983), from whose typology I have chosen what seem to me to be the four central elements, whose topicality can be in little doubt:

- parents' rights versus children's needs
- child saving versus family support
- developmental versus protective services
- in-home versus foster family versus institutional care.

In any era of policy-making all of these dichotomies can be identified, and the powers and duties enshrined in the Children Act 1989 provide merely a snapshot of the ways in which they are currently resolved.

Current problems

The next section highlights some contemporary and more widely publicized examples of both quantitative and qualitative service deficits for children and families. The overview does not purport to be comprehensive; indeed, attempting to produce such a list would be akin to filling the proverbial holed bucket, or painting the Forth Bridge. As we have seen, a key feature of the Children Act 1989 is its codification of legal rights and responsibilities on a perceived continuum along which the various (potential) stages of the child–family–state relationship can be located. That is to say, the Act establishes clear legal requirements for state responsibility towards children (a) in their own homes; (b) out of their own homes, in the care of the state (now referred to as 'looked-after children'); and (c) after they have undergone such a 'looked-after' period. I have taken examples along this continuum in order to examine failure and success in current policy and practice.

Children in their own homes

Section 17, Part III of the Act gives local authorities a general duty to safeguard and promote the welfare of children in need by providing a range and level of services appropriate to their needs. A child is taken to be in need if

(a) he is unlikely to achieve or maintain, or have the opportunity of achieving or maintaining, a reasonable standard of health or development without the provision for him of such services;

(b) his health or development is likely to be significantly impaired, or further impaired, without the provision for him of such services; or

(c) he is disabled.

In addition the Guidance, while stressing the intention that the definition is deliberately wide in order to reinforce the emphasis on preventive support and services, instructs local authorities to 'ascertain the extent of need, and then make decisions about the priorities for service provision'.

The picture of implementation which has so far emerged is mixed. The empirical data are derived substantially from two main sources: a series of research studies commissioned by the Department of Health (Aldgate and Tunstill, 1995; Colton *et al.*, 1995; Tunstill and Aldgate, 1999); and the reports of inspections carried out by the Social Services Inspectorate (SSI) (Social Services Inspectorate, 1997, 1998).

The central finding which has emerged from the studies, and taken up by a range of critics, including the Audit Commission (1994), is the inevitable, although implicit, hierarchy of access to services resulting mainly from the Act's requirement to prioritize, a task, incidentally, undertaken in a period of reduction, or at best, containment of local government spending (unfortunately, of course, alongside the reduction of service entitlement in a range of other state provision, including notably social security).

To put the matter more directly, this means that local authorities have been notably more willing to provide family support services to children seen as being at risk rather than in need. Children seen to be at risk of significant harm or neglect have so far gained access to services more readily than those seen to be 'merely' in need in the community. This second group includes, for example, children living in homes with gas, electricity or water disconnected, children in substandard housing, children with special health needs, children excluded from school, refugee children and children with divorcing parents (Aldgate and Tunstill, 1995).

The 1993 Children Act Report concluded:

> A broadly consistent and somewhat worrying picture is emerging. In general progress towards full implementation of Section 17 ... has been slow. Further work is still needed to provide across the country a range of family services aimed at preventing families reaching the point of breakdown. Some authorities are finding it difficult to move from a reactive social policing role to a more proactive partnership with families. (para. 239, 16)

The general tone of this message has been maintained in SSI and DoH statements about the Act, culminating in the extremely negative findings of the initial Inspection of Services for Children in Need (Department of Health, 1997):

> Decisions were made on a local basis about who should be offered a service and how it should be delivered, often without any assessment process to determine the most appropriate response ... departments were continuing to respond to child protection and looked after child cases to the exclusion of support to other families of children in need ... services continue to be organised as they have been historically. They have not been reviewed to consider whether they meet current needs, how they fit within an overall strategy and whether resources are being used most effectively ... little has been done to counter the negative image that the public have of child care services based on media reports.

However, there are indications that this gloomy picture may be slowly changing for the better; a more recent national research study undertaken by Tunstill and Aldgate (1999) for the Department of Health, based on a sample of 93 families (excluding child protection and disability referrals) in seven local authorities, identified examples of proactive policy and practice, appropriate provision of family support services and a high level of satisfaction on the part of those families who received them. The fact that two-thirds of the families had referred themselves (as opposed to having been referred by professionals) suggests the existence of a rather more user-friendly image of social work and social services departments than the earlier inspection describes. What the study findings do underline is the necessity for distinguishing between 'unsatisfied' and 'dissatisfied' service users, with the former being 'happy' with the nature and quality of the service received but unhappy with the quantity (indeed, in some circumstances insufficient quantity might be no service at all). By comparison, dissatisfied service users might be defined as those for whom neither the nature nor the quality is adequate; in other words, delivering more of the service would not be seen as meeting their needs.

Perhaps the most hopeful message is the feasibility of social services departments meeting parents' needs for the diverse family support services made possible by the 1989 Act, given a synergy between political and professional aspirations in this area. However, the professional contribution can become a reality only if resources are reallocated towards family support in what has become to be called the 'refocusing debate'. The general tenor of this debate, deriving from the research studies outlined above, and in particular from the 1995 Department of Health résumé of sixteen child protection research studies, 'Messages from research', is that children's services should focus on ensuring that child protection is firmly placed within a context of wider work to support families in need.

CHILD PROTECTION

If one discourse has dominated the development of child care policy over the past 20 years then it is the definition, identification and response to the child seen to be *at risk*.

The question of definition lies at the heart of many of the key debates in this area. While there is widespread agreement that child abuse and child protection are socially constructed terms (Parton, 1991; Rogers and Rogers, 1994), this has not prevented the evolution of the concept of a *hierarchy of risk*, which in many ways mirrors the *hierarchy of need* discussed above. As Hill and Tisdall (1997) comment, certain 'risk' situations have been defined as major social problems, whereas others have been marginalized:

> In particular, the notion of child abuse has, apart from a few dissenting voices, been confined to the ill-treatment of children in their own homes and the

concept of child protection has become synonymous with the responses by official agencies to suspected and identified intra-familial abuse.

The current definition of abuse is laid out in *Working Together* (Department of Health and Social Security, 1988): (para. 6.40):

Neglect: The persistent or severe neglect of a child or the failure to protect a child from exposure to any kind of danger, including cold or starvation, or extreme failure to carry out important aspects of care, resulting in significant impairment of the child's health or development, including non-organic failure to thrive.

Physical abuse: Actual or likely physical injury to a child, or failure to prevent physical injury (or suffering) to a child, including deliberate poisoning, suffocation and Münchhausen's syndrome by proxy.

Sexual abuse: Actual or likely sexual exploitation of a child or adolescent. The child may be dependent and/or developmentally immature.

Emotional abuse: Actual or likely severe adverse effect on the emotional and behavioural development of a child caused by persistent or severe emotional ill-treatment or rejection. All abuse involves some emotional ill-treatment. This category is used where it is the main or sole form of abuse.

The evolutionary process through which a definition emerges is itself contentious:

There are moral standpoints about what as a society we will tolerate. There is legislation and guidance which sets out a framework within which professionals should operate and boundaries across which parents should not transgress. Then there is evidence about what is harmful and what is helpful to children. Finally, there is the consumer perspective, that is to say the child's view on what is abusive, or parents' fears for their offspring. Too often, definitions about child protection have reflected one of these dimensions at the expense of others. (Little, 1997, p. 27)

The National Commission of Inquiry into the Prevention of Child Abuse (1996) caused a furore when it proposed the following definition: '*child abuse consists of anything which individuals, institutions or processes do, or fail to do, which directly or indirectly harms or damages the prospects of safe and healthy development into adulthood*'.

Indeed, one possible explanation of the paramountcy of child protection in the scale of social services activity is the equation of a narrow definition with an *apparent* simplicity of the task of measurement, relative to the challenges involved in quantifying need/activity in other areas of work. One manifestation of this 'quantification' approach is the mechanism of the Child Protection Register, a set of nationally collated data which shows that as of 31 March 1996, there were 32,351 children on local registers, the number having fallen from a peak of 45,000 in 1991.

This represents 29 children per 10,000 population aged under 18, a rate decrease of 9 per cent since 1995. There are considerable gender and age variations in respect of the different categories of abuse. Two out of five registrations related to those children considered at risk of physical injury, of whom boys constituted 54 per cent. One third were considered at risk of neglect and 22 per cent at risk of sexual abuse, with girls constituting 61 per cent of this number.

However, over and above the question of how to define abuse, the most sustained criticism of the child protection system within the UK has concerned social services responses, or, to put it rather more emotively, what happens to children and families when they get caught up in the child protection process.

THE RESPONSE PROCESS

A key component in the refocusing debate is estimates, extrapolated from the work of Gibbons *et al.* (1995), of the numbers of children and families involved in the protection process.

Of approximately 11 million children in England (an unknown number of whom may receive 'children in need' services as a result of a stage 1 pre-investigation), around 160,000 are referred to the child protection process. As a result of the first inquiry undertaken, for approximately 40,000 (25 per cent) there is no further investigation. A family visit will be made to 120,000 of these children, resulting in no further investigation for 80,000 (approximately 66 per cent). There will have been emergency separations for about 1500 and a Child Protection Conference will be held for approximately 40,000. Ultimately approximately 24,500 additions will be made to the Register.

By any stretch of the imagination this is an unwieldy system, which has been seen as maximizing the likelihood of harassing and harrying parents, with no compensatory guarantee that supportive services will be forthcoming. It is characterized by legalism and proceduralism (King and Piper, 1990; King and Trowell, 1992), and has been criticized as resulting in mechanical and inspectorial practice by social workers (Holman 1998), whereby the 'primary task of social workers' may become the completion of standard procedures without incurring criticism, rather than the resolution of children's and families' problems' (Jones and Bilton, 1994, p. 32). For Jones and Bilton, the optimum ideals of practice would be based on 'empathy, intuition, imagination and flair, as well as observation, careful analysis, thought and knowledge'.

Farmer (1997, p. 161) concludes:

> The system that has developed is fairly effective at keeping children safe in the short-term, but it has clear limitations in relation to providing for the wider welfare needs of children and their parents. Indeed the emphasis is on short-term

protection to the extent . . . that little attention is paid to providing children with treatment or other help to recover from the harm influenced by the abuse itself and its attendant losses. Yet, when children's and parent's needs were ignored, because of a narrow focus on protection from re-abuse, it is clear that the long-term protection of children from significant harm could not be assured.

Children out of their own homes

The 1989 Act altered traditional terminology in respect of key parts of the child care system, with the expressed intention of changing some of the more unhelpful ways in which both public and professionals conceptualize the care situation: 'So widespread is the misconception that children in care are blameworthy that ultimately they come to accept this stigma themselves' (Page and Clarke, 1977, p. 26).

Under the Act, 'looked-after' children are those subject to a care order (which can be made only by a court) or who are provided with accommodation on a voluntary basis for more than 24 hours. As at 31 March 1996, 51,200 children and young people were being looked after by social services departments in England. In the preceding year 31,900 children started to be looked after while 31,600 ceased to be looked after. The majority of these children (57 per cent) were under care orders, while 40 per cent were looked after by voluntary agreements under Section 20. The most common reasons given for a child starting to be looked after were to give relief to parents or families (29 per cent), abuse or neglect (20 per cent), parent's health (14 per cent), and concern for the child's welfare (8 per cent); other (29 per cent).

There have also been changes in the average length of time for which children are accommodated. Since the implementation of the Children Act in 1991, the average length of time has gradually decreased, from 610 days in 1993 to 500 in 1996. Of children ceasing to be looked after, 19 per cent in 1996 had been looked after for more than two years, compared with 26 per cent in 1993 (Department of Health, 1997).

Perhaps some of the most important trends have been in the *way* children are accommodated. Since 1986, the number of children in local authority homes has substantially decreased, from 13,855 in 1986 to 9710 in 1991 to 5500 in 1996. This represents 11 per cent of children looked after. The number of children looked after in voluntary homes and hostels was 500 in 1996 compared with 1285 in 1986. There were 830 children looked after in privately registered children's homes, a 30 per cent increase in one year. There were 4700 children looked after who were placed with parents, representing 9 per cent of all children looked after. This compares with 6500 (12 per cent) in 1992. Of all children looked after, 2300 (5 per cent) were placed for adoption.

Perhaps the most enduring debate in child placement policy is about the role of fostering. Its positive image was recognized as early as 1896 by the Mundella Report (quoted by Packman, 1975, p. 20):

> Where children are brought up in large institutions the standard of health is lower than that of children living under ordinary conditions ... there is a consensus of opinion that the children have a tendency to be dull, sullen and mechanical.

By contrast, the foster family was thought to be natural and beneficial, and the 1948 Children Act was centrally concerned to bring about the transfer of children from residential care to foster homes, almost along the lines of Stroud's ironic recollections (1960, p. 8):

> There was a tremendous crusading atmosphere ... our impression was ... the country was dotted with castle-like institutions in which hundreds of children dressed in blue serge were drilled to the sound of whistles. We were going to tear down the mouldering bastions.

Such idealism persists, albeit qualified by the consistent findings of empirical studies which have pointed to the increasing difficulty of recruiting foster-carers, due to the increase in the number of women working outside the home; fears of prospective foster-carers that they may be accused of child abuse, the perception that fostering has become much more difficult, and the evidence that foster-carers are inadequately supported by social workers. In addition, the impact of the mixed economy means that private agencies, with higher charges, have begun to usurp the recruitment potential of local authorities.

The 1990s has been dominated by revelations of the sexual, emotional and physical abuse of children in residential care, including a series of high-profile inquiries into abusive regimes, such as 'pindown' in Staffordshire, and the acknowledgement of a lengthy history of abuse in North Wales, culminating in a public inquiry. The clear message to be derived from these scandals is that 'children removed from home avowedly for their own benefit ran the risk of physical, emotional or sexual ill-treatment at the hands of carers' (Hill and Tisdall, 1997, p. 232). Two major Department of Health (Warner, 1992; Utting, 1991) inquiries, chaired respectively by Sir Norman Warner and Sir William Utting, have documented at length the absence of the various safeguards which would protect children from abuse when they are in the care of the state. Less dramatic but of equal concern are the accumulated data on the deficits in the day-to-day lives of separated children, and the fact that the majority of research shows that on average children in care have more behavioural, relationship and educational difficulties than their peers. This is hardly surprising given the summary of data about children in care by Hill and

Tisdall (1997). It includes:

- unplanned and ill-prepared admission
- several moves of home
- several moves of school
- infrequent or no parental contact
- reduced contact with other significant family members
- changes in household composition/roles at home which make it harder for children to fit in
- other children coming and going in the placement
- staff changes in residential care.

A major Department of Health Initiative on Looked After Children is in process and has been widely welcomed and implemented (Ward, 1998). The tide may be turning.

Aftercare

If children and young people survive the period of care itself, then the data on their experiences *after* care are no less depressing. Around 8000 young people leave care annually. One-third leave at age 16 and almost all will have left by 18. Although they represent less than 1 per cent of their age group, they are over-represented in almost every disadvantaged category, as the report from the Action on Aftercare Consortium (1996) describes:

- *education*: more than 75 per cent of care leavers have no educational qualifications. Fewer than 20 per cent continue in full-time education after 16. There are high levels of non-attendance and exclusion from school among 'looked after' children.
- *employment*: between 50 and 80 per cent of care leavers are unemployed.
- offending: 23 per cent of adult and 38 per cent of young prisoners have been in care.
- *homelessness*: Young people who have been 'looked after' are greatly over-represented in the numbers of homeless people.
- *poverty*: Ten per cent of 16- to 17-year-old claimants of Department of Social Security severe hardship payments have been in care.

The picture painted by a 1996 SSI inspection of leaving care services is just as depressing (SSI, 1997). Leaving care services were variable, with examples of good practice alongside areas of concern. Young people themselves had to request further assistance, and although foster-carers provided valuable support, their role was often not formally recognized by the local authority. Available information was patchy, including that on issues of financial support, and young people found it difficult to adjust to living on benefits after relative financial security. Most had been offered a choice of accommodation, but some felt isolated, and concerned about being housed in unsafe areas. There were particular problems in obtaining mental health services. Few young people were able to find a job. Disabled young people experienced particular difficulties in moving from child to adult services.

Conclusion

The data discussed above appear to confirm the failure of social services departments to fulfil their responsibilities in respect of children and young people. It is difficult to deny, that as currently organized, the departments constitute as much a part of the problem as the answer. However, the issues which threaten a positive response to the needs of children and young people are complex and go far beyond organizational effectiveness. They are bound up with questions about the nature of the relationship between child, family and state, and beyond that with ultimate models of equality and social justice. More specifically, as I argued at the beginning of this chapter, the history of social services departments is best explored within the context of three key themes: the organizational tradition, the familiarization of childhood and the uneasy relationship with universal provision.

All three are obvious in the current policy debate. For example, if we take the failure of social services departments to safeguard the welfare of children within the formal care system, then many of the issues are associated with organizational deficits. While not all problems can be laid at the organizational door, matters such as unplanned admission, placement moves, inadequate educational provision and flawed staff recruitment policy could all be minimized, if not avoided, by the introduction of child-sensitive and organizationally meticulous procedures. The same analysis may well apply to the failure of social services to move away from a narrow focus on child protection towards a broader concern with children in need.

The Seventh Annual Report of the Chief Inspector, Social Services Inspectorate (Department of Health, 1998), highlights five themes which all, to a greater or lesser extent, relate to social services departments as *organizations*, by asking if they currently:

1. involve service users and encourage independence;
2. assess risks to vulnerable children and adults and protect them;
3. are organized to deliver good-quality as well as economic services;
4. work with other agencies to jointly plan and deliver services;
5. select, train and manage their workforce well.

The report concludes that social services departments are failing to provide proper services because they lack strategic direction and their management is seriously flawed. It is considerably more critical of the poor management of children's as opposed to adult services, and the consequent poor planning and decision-making for children in care and those in need. As a result, families needing support are being caught up in the child protection system. There are long delays for placements and an absence of care plans and key workers. As regards the safeguarding of children, the report concludes that most departments are failing to provide the full range of safeguards, although most have now implemented the recommendations of the Warner Report on the recruitment and vetting of staff.

The final message of the 1998 Report is that while some social services managers regard new policy initiatives (such as council-wide strategies, early excellence policies, and health and education action zones) as additional burdens, such an attitude fails to recognize the major contribution which social services have to make to the wider agenda. Sir Herbert Laming, author of the report, when interviewed after its publication, declared:

> We are thrilled by seeing examples of quite excellent commitment, skill, compassion and courage in difficult situations, but there are situations of intense frustration and anger that vulnerable people have been left exposed to an unacceptable risk and often abuse … management means management. By that I mean setting standards, having procedures, making sure that these standards are translated into action and having regular supervision and reviews.

However, while this litany of criticism must be addressed and although it is undeniably based largely on empirical data, it is only one item on the charge sheet in respect of social services. The tenor of the statements from politicians about the future of social services is less specific and/or objective, and illustrates the persistent influence of two other themes identified at the outset – the familiarization of childhood and an uneasy relationship with universal provision.

Much of current New Labour policy stresses the centrality of the family unit; in this it is largely indistinguishable from that of the previous Conservative administration. However, there are suggestions in some policy statements of a growing emphasis on the responsibilities of the family as opposed to those of the state, and in particular on the family's culpability for the transgressions of children and young people. There are strong indications that social services departments will need to adjust to opposing policy directions in other areas of government over which they have little or no control, and which may be at considerable variance with their own mandate.

For example, a constant theme in current policy discussions around children and young people has been the link between criminal and antisocial behaviour and the absence of satisfactory parenting experiences. The statements of Jack Straw, Home Secretary, have stressed this connection. Indeed, the Parenting Orders introduced by Straw in the 1998 Crime and Disorder Act will *compel* parents to undertake parental skills education. Similarly, in 1997 Paul Boateng (then junior health minister) told social services directors:

> Childhood throws up a variety of needs that all children experience. I want to broaden the scope of the Department of Health's current refocussing initiative beyond family support and child protection to embrace parenting as a whole. It means looking at issues of parenting not simply in terms of family support, if by that you mean intervention where parents are believed to be failing. Parenting skills are something which everyone can tap into without stigma.

Another example is the government's stress on the moral and social worth of employment (in programmes such as welfare to work and the 'new deal' for lone parents), so that some critics have seen a danger of its taking precedence over other considerations such as the care of children.

For some commentators (of whom Donzelot (1979) would certainly be one) these developments serve to underline the negative aspects of the fusion of childhood into the family institution (the familiarization of childhood) and to demonstrate the way in which the family is itself vulnerable to control by the state. Undeniably, at a practical rather than theoretical level, new policies in other areas complicate the task for social services departments as currently constituted.

Lastly, the tone of current welfare debates has served to highlight what I have called the uneasy relationship within which (selectivist) social services departments have coexisted with other universalist aspects of the welfare system. The uncertainty of New Labour as to where the boundary between selectivity and universalism should be drawn is illustrated by the following statement (Boateng, 1997):

> I want families and vulnerable people to be working with social services, to be served by social services. For each and every one of them, I want there to be a plan that means there will come a time when social services will not be in their lives at all ... we want those engaged in social care to be agents of change in the lives of those they are working with, to and alongside. It's not just about picking up the extremes of society's casualties: it's about providing a much broader service.

The contradictions in this statement can be illustrated by two examples. What bedevils the adequate delivery of family support services within the 1989 Children Act is as much the level of resources made available through public spending allocations to other departments such as social security and housing local authorities, as the professional competence or indeed incompetence of social workers. What aggravates the narrow focus of child abuse work is the reluctance of politicians, acting on behalf of the public, to evince the same horror at material and environmental threats to children's welfare as the culpable actions of individual parents and carers. The young people who go from care to homelessness and unemployment, with few educational qualifications, reflect both the impermeability of the boundary between *selectivity* in the personal social services and *universality* in education, and of course within social security provision, given the removal of benefits for young people following the 1986 Social Security Act. As Willis (1998, p. 5) has commented:

> Herein lies the choice for those who wish to shape the strategic agenda for the personal social services. Is its role to be focused solely on people who are unable or unwilling to accept Labour's new contract of social responsibility – to ensure that vulnerable children are cared for ... or is it to have a wider role in the task of building community support for an agenda that may range from tackling social and economic decline, to building a new tram system, to tackling drug abuse, to improving education and training standards, to protecting the environment, to developing centres of excellence for the arts and recreation, to revitalising town centres?

The future

So what may be a way forward which takes account of the realities of the needs of children, young people and families, and yet maintains the positive aspects of current provision? There are several key dimensions along which choice of new policy directions could be made. They include the public/voluntary/private divide, the generic versus the specialist model and provision targeted at *children* versus provision targeted at *families.* Each has its adherents and, on the basis of the experience of the last century at least, it would be difficult to espouse one monolithic set of ideologies or structures as the guarantor of 'good' standards. This chapter does not permit the delineation of an optimum strategy, but there are clear indications of the shape of the drawing-board upon which political and professional architects of provision will operate.

At the level of organizational structures the family centre currently enjoys wide and enthusiastic support as a possible means of delivering services:

> The idea of a 'primary resource' or the 'one-stop-shop family centre could act as a single point of entry to a range of multi-agency support services such as drop-in facilities, peer support groups, nursery, benefits and housing advice, child health and well women clinics, playgroups, and after school schemes. Such a model would help to destigmatise social services support – a current

problem – but would not exclude access to a social worker if requested or required. (Audit Commission, Executive Summary, 1994, p. 15)

However, at the time of writing, it is more than likely that the forthcoming debate will be as much an ideological as an organizational one; we will only know in the future whether the recent declamations of politicians are the first shots in a new battle to give children a genuinely better deal from society through the mechanism of social services (or, where appropriate, other departments), or merely the closing rounds in a long-running but diversionary war against social services departments as organizations, in which they have been held as hostages by society's ambivalent commitment to meeting the needs of children and young people.

References

Aldgate, J. and Tunstill, J. (1995) Making sense of Section 17: implementing services for children in need within the 1989 Children Act. London: HMSO.

Aldgate, J. *et al.* (1998) Postgraduate certificate in supervision and mentoring (child care) Unit 3. School of Social Work, Leicester University.

Audit Commission (1994) Seen but not heard: local authority and child health services. London: HMSO.

Boateng, P. (1997) Speech to DoH conference: Effective Senior Management Development. London.

Brannen, J. and O'Brien, M. (eds) (1996) *Children in Families: Research and Policy*. London: Falmer.

Colton, M., Drury, C. and Williams, M. (1995) Children in need: definition, identification and support. *British Journal of Social Work*, 25, 711–28.

Cunningham, H. (1995) *Children and Childhood in Western Society since 1500*. Oxford: Oxford University Press.

Department of Health (1990a) An introduction to the Children Act 1989. London: HMSO.

Department of Health (1990b) Principles in practice in guidance and regulations. London: HMSO.

Department of Health (1995) Child protection: messages from research. London: HMSO.

Department of Health (1997) Children looked after by local authorities, year ending 31st March 1996. London: HMSO.

Department of Health (1998) Social services facing the future: the seventh annual report of the Chief Inspectorate 1997/98. London: Stationery Office.

DHSS (1985a) Review of child care law: report to Ministers of an inter-departmental working party. London: HMSO.

DHSS (1985b) Social work decisions in child care. London: HMSO.

Department of Health and Social Security (1988) Working together: a guide to interagency co-operation for the protection of children from abuse. London: HMSO.

Donzelot, J. (1979) *The Policing of Families: Welfare versus the State.* London: Hutchinson.

Farmer, E. (1997) Protection and child welfare: striking the balance. In N. Parton (ed.), *Governing the Family*, pp. 146–65. London: Macmillan.

Fox Harding, L. (1991) *Perspectives in Child Care Policy.* Harlow: Longman.

Fox Harding, L. (1996) *Family, State and Social Policy.* London: Macmillan.

Gibbons, J., Conroy, S. and Bell, C. (1995) *Operating the Child Protection System: A Study of Child Protection Practices in English Local Authorities.* London: HMSO.

Hardiker, P., Exton, K. and Barker, M. (1991) *Policies and Practices in Preventive Child Care.* Aldershot: Avebury.

Hendrick, H. (1997) *Children, Childhood and English Society, 1880–1990.* Cambridge: Cambridge University Press.

Heywood, J. (1978) *Children in Care: The Development of the Service for the Deprived Child.* London: Routledge and Kegan Paul.

Hill, M. (1997) *The Policy Process in the Modern State.* Hemel Hempstead: Harvester Wheatsheaf.

Hill, M. and Tisdall, K. (1997) *Children and Society.* Harlow: Longman.

Holman, B. (1998) *Putting Families First: Prevention and Child Care.* London: Macmillan.

Illich, I. (1975) *Medical Nemesis.* New York: Harper & Row.

James, A. and Prout, A. (eds) (1990) *Constructing and Reconstructing Childhood: Contemporary Issues in the Sociological Study of Childhood.* London: Falmer Press.

Jones, A. and Bilton, K. (1994) *The Shape of Children's Services.* London: The National Children's Bureau.

King, M. and Piper, C. (1990) *How the Law Thinks about Children.* Aldershot: Gower.

King, M. and Trowell, J. (1992) *Children's Welfare and the Law: The Limits of Legal Intervention.* London: Sage.

Laming, H. (1998) interviewed in *Community Care*, 25 June, p. 10.

Little, M. (1997) The re-focussing of children's services: the contribution of research. In N. Parton (ed.), *Child Protection and Family Support.* London: Routledge.

McGowan, B. (1983) Historical evolution of child welfare services. In B. McGowan and W. Meezan (eds), *Child Welfare: Current Dilemmas, Future Directions*, pp. 45–93. Itasca, IL: Peacock.

Millar, J. and Warman, A. (1996) *Family Obligations in Europe*. London: Family Policy Studies Centre.

National Commission of Inquiry into the Prevention of Child Abuse. (1996) Childhood Matters. London: National Society for the Prevention of Cruelty to Children.

Packman, J. (1975) *The Child's Generation*. Oxford: Blackwell.

Page, R. and Clarke, G. (eds) (1977) *Who Cares? Young People in Care Speak Out*. London: National Children's Bureau.

Parker, R.A. (1980) *Caring for Separated Children*. London: Macmillan.

Parton, N. (1991) *Governing the Family*. London: Macmillan.

Rogers, R.S. and Rogers, W.S. (1994) *Stories of Childhood*. Toronto: University of Toronto Press.

Royal College of Physicians (1988) Medical Care of the Newborn in England and Wales. Report of a working party. London: RCP.

Seebohm Report (1968) The report of the Committee on Local Authority and Allied Personal Social Services. Cmnd. 3703. London: HMSO.

Social Services Inspectorate (1997) Responding to families in need: inspection of assessment, planning and decision making in family support services. London: Department of Health.

Social Services Inspectorate (1998) *Partners in Planning: Approaches to Planning Services for Children and their Families*. London: DoH

Stevenson, O. (1997) 50 years of services to children in need of care. Lucy Faithfull Memorial Lecture. Barkingside: Barnardos.

Stroud, J. (1960) *The Shorn Lamb*. London: Longman.

Tunstill, J. (1997) Implementing the family support clauses of the 1989 Children Act: legislative, professional and organisational obstacles. In N. Parton (ed.), *Child Protection and Family Support: Tensions, Contradictions and Possibilities*. London: Routledge.

Tunstill, J. and Aldgate, J. (1999) Children in need: policy into practice. London: HMSO.

Utting, W. (1991) *Children in Public Care: A Review of Residential Care*. London: HMSO.

Ward, H. (1998) Using a child development model to assess the outcomes of social work interventions with families. *Children and Society*, **12** (3), 202–11.

Warner, N. (1992) Choosing with Care: Report of the Committee Inquiry into the Selection, *Development and Management of Staff in Children's Homes*. London: HMSO.

Wilding, P. (1992) The public sector in the 1990s. In *Social Policy Review*, no. 4. Social Policy Association. Canterbury: University of Kent.

Willis, M. (1998) Personal social services 1998–2002. shaping the strategic agenda: issues and opportunities. Inlogov Seminar, 21 April, Birmingham.

8

Murder by children: principles for a preventive strategy

Stewart Asquith and Elizabeth Cutting

The conviction in 1993 of two young boys both just over the age of criminal responsibility (10 in England and Wales) for the murder of the toddler James Bulger prompted widespread public and political debate (not only in the UK but further afield in the wider international arena) as to the most appropriate means of dealing with children who kill.

In particular, questions were asked about the kinds of explanations for murder by children and whether there was any evidence of an increase in the number of such murders. The validity of the age of criminal responsibility as it applied to the two boys who killed James Bulger and the implications for two young boys of being dealt with in what was effectively a court of criminal law were also critically examined. The nature of parenting and the support provided to parents whose children could be deemed to be at risk was identified as a crucial element in both explaining why the two boys had done what they did and in providing the basis for a means whereby such horrific occurrences could be prevented. The appropriateness of the punishment (and quite severe punishment at that) and the need to consider the welfare of the two boys once again was a source of conflict. In short, the very philosophy on which the UK juvenile justice systems are based was subjected to critical scrutiny, and the strength of a punitive response to such cases was graphically manifested for all to witness when groups of adults beat on the courtroom doors and on the vans carrying the two boys from court, some demanding that they be locked up for life, others that capital punishment should be brought back for such cases.

The significance of the Bulger case, and other cases of murder by children, was that it provoked a fundamental questioning both by the public and by politicians about the very principles on which systems of juvenile justice are based. The implications of such a fundamental reappraisal of the very philosophy on which our approach to dealing with children who commit offences (particularly those who commit serious offences) reverberated around Europe, including Central and Eastern Europe (Asquith, 1996). Systems of juvenile justice generally deal with large numbers of children who commit the less serious offences – usually property offences, including theft, damage, burglary, etc. Such offences have characterized the history of juvenile justice systems, and it has also been the case that the significant developments in juvenile justice systems have occurred in response to the need to deal with serious cases such as the Bulger case.

What all of the more serious cases posed were of course fundamental dilemmas for any system of juvenile justice: whether to be more concerned about the offence committed or about the child or young person who had committed it; whether to punish or be concerned about the welfare of the offender; whether to employ a court-based system of proceedings or a less judicially oriented process; whether to hold children criminally responsible or not. What is also clear in the wake of the Bulger case is that there was and still is a fundamental lack of agreement as to what measures are most appropriate to deal with children such as the two boys who killed James Bulger.

Nor is this just a matter of concern for those children who commit the most serious offences as we continue to promote practices and policies in relation to the young whose value and efficacy has to be in question. Included among these must surely be the apparent appeal of electronic tagging for those who have offended and the use of curfews which apply to all children whether they have offended or not.

More often than not, developments in juvenile justice and in the measures for young offenders (particularly where the offences are serious ones) are a response to public or political will. They are rarely influenced by research and evidence. This is an argument that has, of course, developed elsewhere in advocating what has been referred to as an evidence-based approach to the prevention of offending by children and young people. By this is meant, very simply, the importance of basing developments in juvenile justice on available evidence about the causes of offending behaviour, the appropriateness of different forms of proceedings, and the merits of different types of measures.

What also characterizes developments in juvenile justice which derive from public and political responses to serious cases is that they are designed to deal with those children who have already offended. Furthermore, where 'preventive' strategies are proposed, these more often than not relate to the need to prevent reoffending by children or young people. Only now is attention being focused on preventing children being at risk of becoming an offender in the first place. This approach has serious implications for the redistribution of resources away from dealing with those who commit offences to the development of a strategy which seeks to address those factors that increase the risk that they will become offenders.

In this chapter, we intend to explore the evidence available which might be used in providing principles on which to base a strategy for the prevention of serious offending (including murder) by children and young people. By a preventive strategy we mean a strategy which has as its prime objective the reduction of the risk that a child will at some stage in his or her life commit a serious offence. The focus for a truly preventive strategy is those factors which put a child at risk of becoming an offender. There is considerable research evidence which identifies the importance of early intervention in the lives of children in order to prevent them being at risk of offending later in life.

Our argument here is that this applies as much to those who commit serious offences as it does to those who commit the vast majority of offences dealt with by our juvenile justice systems. It is the more serious cases which provide the most stringent test of the principles on which a system of justice for children who offend is based. Our argument will be that we do have available knowledge about and explanations for serious offending which can provide the framework for an effective preventive strategy.

A statement by an American psychologist sums up our position neatly. In referring to those factors which may account for serious violence, he says: 'Violence does not drop out of the sky at age fifteen. It is part of a long developmental process that begins in early childhood' (Thornberry, 1994, p. 4). The implication of such a position is that if we continue to focus our attention on those children who have indeed offended and been caught up in the formal system of control, then we will continue to fail to address those very factors which we know have contributed to their behaviour.

The UK, along with most countries in the world, has ratified the United Nations Convention on the Rights of the Child, which presents a package of minimum guidelines on which are to be based all practices and policies relating to British children. The convention provides a suitable conceptual framework on which to base a strategy for preventing offending (including serious offending) by addressing the life experiences of all children.

Murder by children and young people

Questions such as 'Is there an increase in murder by children and young people?', simple as they are in the asking, are far from simple in terms of clear and easy answers. This is particularly the case if we take into consideration information and evidence from other countries. The merit of such cross-country comparison is, of course, that it allows us to examine critically the premises and principles on which our own responses to murder by children and young people are based. Most countries, certainly those in Europe, are currently reviewing their system of juvenile justice, and the committal of murder by children and young people undoubtedly has a major effect on proposals for future developments in juvenile justice. Whether or not there has been an increase in murder by children and young people, it is clear that such crimes occupy a central position in public and political consciousness. The danger is, of course, that the measures developed may bear little relationship to the actual levels of murder by children and young people. The tendency to categorize children into two distinct camps – angels or devils – further fuels the fear of the extreme threats some children may pose for us.

Two broad comments can be made on the basis of the evidence available in the literature. One is that whereas there appears to have been a general reduction in juvenile delinquency in Western Europe in the past five years, there has been a slight increase in the numbers of offences involving violence by children and young people (see Asquith, 1992; Walgrave, 1996, in reference to Western Europe generally).

In Central and Eastern Europe, the rates of juvenile delinquency have generally increased, very much reflecting countries in transition, with serious concern expressed about the increase in offences of violence involving children and young people, and their use of weapons (Asquith, 1996). Nevertheless, although the figures reveal a dramatic increase in offending by children and young people, there is general recognition that rates of delinquency and offending have not yet reached levels associated with Western Europe. What concerns our East European colleagues is, first, the rate of the increase more than the fact of an increase itself and, second, the qualitative change in the nature of violent offences. In particular, offences of violence appear to display greater degrees of seriousness and harm (Asquith, 1996).

As for the situation in the US, the growth of the 'abolitionist' movement, which seeks the abolition of a distinctive process for young offenders, is in part based on the apparent increase in serious offences by children and young. What the abolitionists argue is that the fact that the offender is a child should not mean that he or she receives any more lenient or favourable treatment than adults who offend – particularly where the offences involve violence or murder. Thus, there should be no special court or procedure for such children since the main concern rests with the offence they have committed, not with their status as children. Juvenile courts should be abolished. It is not difficult to link the sentiments behind this argument with the demands that the boys who killed James Bulger should be exposed to the full rigours of the criminal law and penal measures.

The other is that despite the increasing concern expressed in Western Europe about the numbers of murders by children and young people, it does not appear to be the case that there is any substantial increase, if any increase at all. In reference to the UK, Cavadino (1996) argues that there has been no increase. Commenting on the situation in Western Europe in general, Walgrave (1996) asserts that the figures may well reveal a degree of stability.

The picture as regards Central and Eastern Europe is, however, very different. Just as there is a dramatic increase in the levels of offending by children and young people generally (Asquith, 1996), so there is a significant increase in a number of countries in the numbers of murders committed by children and young people. A number of things have to be said here. One is that the murders by children and young people in the UK do not, at least on the evidence available to us, involve the use of weapons, whereas a prime characteristic of murders by children and young people in a number of countries in Central and Eastern Europe is that they do involve weapons (such as pistols and rifles) and appear to be associated with other crimes such as robberies. Moreover, again on the available evidence, they reflect group organization and planning. Indeed, on occasion children have been contracted to kill.

The general principle that can be drawn, though, from even a cursory examination of the situation in Central and Eastern Europe is that offending by children and young people, including serious offending such as murder, has to be articulated with much broader social concerns. Killing by children cannot be divorced from the social contexts and the life experiences they have undergone. To ignore such considerations would be to emphasize notions of 'evil' and 'wickedness' as manifested during the Bulger trial and other trials involving children. It would also serve to perpetuate the myth that children can be broken down into two distinct categories: the angels and the devils. It would be inexcusable to explain the killing by children caught up in situations of armed conflict in many parts of the world without making reference to the specific circumstances of those children who 'become' soldiers. Our argument here is that it must also be inexcusable for a society such as our own to ignore the contribution of family, social and community considerations in seeking to explain, and thereby respond to, killing by children. If we do, then we must surely be rightly accused of blaming those who themselves may be victims.

What we also know from literature relating to the US is that increasing rates of homicide by children and young people – to which the abolitionist movement referred to above is but one form of response – have reached what have been described as alarming levels. Wilson and Howell (1995) argue that chronic, serious and violent juvenile delinquency is increasing and is likely to continue to do so. Referring to work undertaken by the

Federal Bureau of Investigation relating to 1993, Wilson and Howell go on to show that juveniles committed 13 per cent of all violent crimes (homicides, rapes, robberies and aggravated assaults) in the US. Juveniles were responsible for 9 per cent of all murder clearances, 14 per cent of forcible rapes, 17 per cent of robberies and 13 per cent of all aggravated assaults.

Above, we suggested that the use of weapons was an important factor in the equation when seeking to present a profile of murder by children in Central and Eastern Europe. Exactly the same can be said of the US. In comparing the experience of many children in areas in which the gun culture is prevalent with those children in war zones around the world, Garbarino and Kostelny (1996) emphasize the need to recognize the fact that in a culture of violence, children not only may be at risk of being guilty of homicide but also may be at great risk of being the victims.

In terms of the influence of weapons, Garbarino and Kostelny point to two things. One is that as the technology of weaponry changes so does the nature of homicides, including those by children and young people. A quotation from their work graphically illustrates this:

> Data from Chicago's Cook County Hospital provide another perspective on the changing nature of violence facing children in America. In 1982, the hospital responded to approximately 500 gunshot cases. In 1992, the number was approximately 1,000. However, in 1982 almost all these cases involved single bullet injuries, while in 1992, 25% involved multiple bullets. (Garbrino and Kostelney, 1996, p. 92)

And in identifying the significance of the availability of weapons on children's world views they again graphically note:

> Perhaps a few examples will help illuminate the effects of this gun culture on the experience of childhood. In Detroit, a young boy whose idolised teenage brother was killed in a gang-related attack was asked, 'If you could have anything in the whole world, what would it be?' His answer: 'A gun so I could blow away the person that killed my brother' (Marin, 1988). In California, when we asked a nine-year-old boy living in a neighbourhood characterised by declining security 'What would it take to make you feel safer here?' he replied simply, 'If I had a gun of my own.' In a middle-class suburb of Chicago, when we asked a classroom of eight-year-olds, 'If you needed a gun could you get one?' a third of the children were able to describe in detail how they would get one. In a prison in North Carolina, when we asked three incarcerated teenagers about why they had done the shooting that had landed them in prison, all three replied, 'What else was I supposed to do?' (Garbarino and Kostelny, 1996, p. 94)

Garbarino and Kostelny's comments reflect the conclusions drawn by other commentators who point to the relationship between the numbers of homicides committed by children and young people and the fact that many of the victims are themselves young. This is graphically described in the following quotation:

> 'Mom, can I tell you something? I'm worried. All of the boys I grew up with are dead.... What am I supposed to do?' The question was from a thirteen-year-old boy in New Orleans. His mother suddenly realised that, of a group of six-year-olds who had started school together seven years earlier, only her son was still living. All the others had met violent deaths. (Thornbery, 1994).

The value of Garbarino and Kostelny's work for our purpose is that it emphasizes the significance of social circumstances and life experiences which put children at risk of becoming serious offenders. This is generally ignored in the literature, which tends to focus on the individual in terms of pathological disturbance.

Docherty, for example, points out that there is generally very little information in the UK on children who kill and that such information as is available is generally based on a case study approach to analysis, which further inhibits an accurate assessment of the extent of such behaviours (Docherty, 1997). He also points out is that there is generally very little information available on children in the UK who have been convicted of murder. Most of the literature in the field is in fact American.

The main point to make here is that whereas offending by children and young people in Western Europe does appear to be generally on the decrease, it is the social and political reaction to that small group of young offenders who commit the more serious crimes, including murder, which influences the debates and arguments about the future direction of juvenile justice.

Docherty (1997) is able, though, to point to the fact that of all murders committed in the mid-1980s in the US, 7 per cent were committed by adolescents (those between 10 and 17), surely a much higher figure than for the UK or Western Europe in general. As we shall see, the literature on murder by children tends to be psychiatrically oriented and mostly American. The question that Docherty rightly raises is whether inferences drawn from primarily American material can be applied to the UK context. Implicit, of course, is the argument that they cannot and that there is great need for studies of murder by children and young people, as of violent offences generally, to be conducted in a specifically UK context. The concern must be, though, the extent to which what is happening in an American context anticipates developments in the UK. In terms of the nature of the response to serious offending by children and young people, the history of juvenile justice in the UK is that it has been influenced greatly by events and developments in the US, particularly where serious offences have been committed.

But in general terms, the answer to the question of whether there has been an increase in the rates of murder by children and young people has to be that it depends on which country or jurisdiction is being discussed. As far as the UK and Western Europe are concerned, it can confidently be stated that there is little evidence of any increase in such behaviours. But as Bailleau (1996) argues, whether such offences have increased or not is in many respects less important than the level of fear or insecurity reflected in the public consciousness about the potential threats posed by children and young people. Boswell (1995) also argues that there is no evidence of any increase in murder by children. However, there is evidence, she argues, of a change in the way in which we respond to murder by children when it does occur:

> Child and adolescent murder is not new; it has manifested itself through the ages and has often been dealt with more humanely than the present punitive penological climate would allow.

> [T]he law has never quite worked out how to deal with this small but singular group of children who shatter children's warm images of laughter, play and innocence. [such children] are hostages to the fortune of its interpretations on each and every occasion that their grave crimes are processed through the adult criminal courts. (Boswell, 1995, p. 23).

Age of criminal responsibility

England, Wales and Scotland have among the lowest ages of criminal responsibility in the world (see Table 8.1). Concern was expressed at the fact that the two boys who killed James Bulger, because they were just above the age of criminal responsibility (10), experienced the whole gamut of prosecution under criminal law in an adversarial courtroom scenario. It could be argued (see Asquith, 1996) that children under 14 who are charged with murder should not be liable for public trial in adult criminal courts and, for those between 14 and 18, public hearings may be held but with reporting restrictions. Cavadino (1996) also argued that the system of juvenile justice in England and Wales is far more punitive than in the rest of Europe; it fails to meet the needs of disturbed juveniles and fails to provide the treatment which these young people require to overcome their violent tendencies. The paradox is, as we shall argue when we consider the explanations offered by children and young people, that those children who are most in need of help and treatment may well not receive it from a juvenile justice system driven more by the seriousness of the offence than by the seriousness of the need.

The decision as to how to deal with those children who commit serious

Table 8.1 Age of criminal responsibility (Asquith 1996)

Country	Age
Austria	14
Belgium	18
Bulgaria	14
Czech Republic	15
Croatia	14
England/Wales	10
Estonia	15 but may be lowered to 13
France	13
Germany	14
Hungary	14
Ireland	7
Latvia	16 but may be lowered to 14
Liechtenstein	7
Macedonia	16 but may be lowered to 14
Moldova	16 but may be lowered to 14
Poland	17 but may be lowered to 16
Portugal	16
Russia	16 but may be lowered to 14
Scandinavian countries (all)	15
Scotland	8
Slovak Republic	15
Slovenia	14
Spain	16
Switzerland	7
Ukraine	16 but may be lowered to 14

offences is ultimately both a moral and a political one. Nevertheless, if we do have evidence about those factors which put children at risk of becoming serious offenders, and if we ignore these in the development of strategies and practices, then we must surely fail to prevent that very behaviour we are concerned with.

The age of criminal responsibility varies greatly across Europe with England and Wales and Scotland having among the lowest ages of criminal responsibility (Table 8.1).

As noted elsewhere (Asquith, 1998), in a number of countries the age of criminal responsibility may be lowered in reference to the commission of certain offences, particularly serious offences. For example, in Estonia the age of criminal responsibility is 15 but it may be lowered to 13 for serious offences such as homicide; in Poland the age is 17 but again it may be lowered (or indeed raised by one year). In Latvia, Macedonia, Moldova,

Russia and Ukraine the age of criminal responsibility is set at 16 but again may be lowered to 14 for particularly serious offences.

But the general inference to be drawn is that the age of criminal responsibility is much higher than in the UK. The relevance of this is, of course, not simply about the age at which we think children should be held criminally responsible; it articulates with much broader concerns about children, notions of childhood and the competencies we ascribe to children. The legal system, through key concepts such as criminal responsibility, embodies assumptions and values about children and childhood which reflect wider social values. The Bulger case touched on wider issues than juvenile justice and in particular forced us to ask what status we give to children and how we as adults, either as individuals or through our major institutions, relate to them.

The issue is whether in the wake of the Bulger case and others involving murder, or serious offending, by children and young people, the age of criminal responsibility in the UK is to be addressed. The difficulty is, of course, whether alterations can be made to the age of criminal responsibility without addressing other elements in the system we employ for dealing with those children who commit serious offences. The danger of the abolitionist movement, for example, is that there is no felt need to alter the age of criminal responsibility precisely because children who kill or commit violent offences should be punished and subjected to the full panoply of the criminal law. Conversely, the argument for the raising of the age of criminal responsibility is often made in the context of a commitment to a welfare approach to dealing with those children who commit offences.

The concern with the low age of criminal responsibility in the UK is, of course, that young children may not have the necessary mental and cognitive capacities to be truly capable of being held responsible for what they have done. What we shall also see from the current literature is that factors can be identified in the background of those children who commit serious offences which clearly explain their behaviour and at the same time provide the basis for a means of preventing it. Such offenders can be seen more as victims, themselves in need of help and support.

The fact that the age of criminal responsibility is so low in the UK in part logically implied that the two boys who murdered James Bulger had to go through some form of criminal procedure and must surely have influenced any move to ensure that the boys would be held in custody for a long time.

Murder by children: the search for explanations

Garbarino and Kostelny (1996), in drawing parallels between children in war zones and the experience of many children in American cities, make an implicit general point in their work: that to understand why a child kills, we have to understand something about the life experiences of that child. There are psychological, family, social and political contexts which have to be taken into account in any attempt to understand just what it is that allows a child to kill. This applies as much to those children who find themselves involved in civil and political armed conflict as it does to the children who killed James Bulger.

What every review of the literature on children who kill reveals is that there are a number of constancies or common elements to the explanations offered concerning such an extreme behaviour. These will include

- negative early life experiences
- disadvantage
- abuse, physical or sexual
- violence
- punitive childrearing practices.

We do not suggest that any one of these factors will necessarily in and of itself put children at risk of becoming an offender. Rather, where more than one of these factors are experienced, the multiple effect increases the likelihood that a child will offend later in life. What has also been suggested, of course, is that precisely the same set of circumstances may well put children at risk of being abused and that strategies which fail to address such life experiences will fail to prevent the experience of abuse for many of our children (Childhood Matters, 1996).

But in terms of those children who kill, such factors are identified as crucial by a number of commentators. Wilson and Howell, for example, in referring to the situation in the US, claim that a small proportion of juveniles account for the bulk of serious offences and point to the factors which push young people towards such behaviour. They state that the links between social conditions, availability of weapons, child abuse and neglect, and later serious violent offending offer an additional challenge for delinquency prevention and intervention programmes. Such offenders are the product of complex, co-occurring, multiple problems which require comprehensive solutions if the current upward trend in the US is to be addressed. Garbarino and Kostelny (1996) likewise point to the effects of violence on children's development and how the experience of living in a violent culture, and a gun culture, has an undoubted effect on the early life experiences of children.

In relation to the UK, it is also now recognized that violence by children in general is inextricably linked to violence to them, and that most of the identified determinant factors are controlled by adults (Children and Violence, 1995). There is an increasing acceptance of social explanations of offending behaviour which locate the causes of delinquency in the family, social or community background of the young child. This has clear implications for the involvement of wider policy initiatives in the prevention of delinquency and serious offending by children and young people. It is clear that if we can explain delinquency and serious offending by social factors, and in particular those factors which impinge on the early life experiences of children, then we can no longer expect our juvenile justice system alone to solve the problem of delinquency and particularly that of serious offending.

The Gulbenkian Commission (Children and Violence, 1995) conducted a comprehensive review of research and sought the opinions and views of a wide range of organizations and individuals from a number of countries with a view to identifying those factors associated with people becoming violent. Thus its conclusions both reflect and confirm, from a wider constituency, the information from the academic community. This in itself reflects a convergence of views that punishment, and indeed welfare or educative measures applied later in the life of an offender, may not be the most effective means of dealing with violent behaviour which appears to have its roots in early life experiences.

There has been a general shift, apparent in the international literature, to the need to identify those early-life factors and experiences which put children at risk of serious offending later in life. This has, of course, obvious implications for the development of appropriate policies and practices.

A recent review of the backgrounds of a large sample of children in England and Wales who have killed or committed other serious (usually violent) crimes showed that 72 per cent had experienced abuse of some form and 53 per cent had experienced significant loss (death or loss of contact with someone important) (Boswell, 1995). In all, 35 per cent had experienced both, and a total of 91 per cent had experienced at least one. The results of this study echo similar studies in a number of different countries (see Docherty, 1997) and clearly point to the significance of the family in influencing children's behaviour. While there is no direct correlation between the presence or absence of these factors in determining whether a child is likely to behave violently, it is difficult to ignore the influence of these experiences on development.

What most of the available studies also show is that the experiences of children in families where their life experiences are potentially negative may well be exaggerated by the influence of other factors in their social context such as poverty, unemployment, alcohol abuse and so on.

Other relevant factors identified as significant in the risk of a child's becoming violent are parental mental illness, parental rejection, exposure to repetitive or extreme violence (including witnessing such violence), neurological abnormalities, drug and alcohol abuse, and in some cases mental illness. The existence of these factors does not necessarily lead to the development of a violent child, but in certain cases the conjunction of such factors with other circumstances (such as the friendship of two young people with complementary disturbed personalities, or in adolescence the escalation of behaviour through gang participation) can result in serious violent acts which otherwise might not have taken place (Cavadino, 1996).

What is evident from the literature is that negative early life experiences not only can account for offending in later life but, from all the available evidence, also can account for serious offending including murder. Docherty's review (1997) of parricide in the US and Canada confirms the importance of Boswell's work in identifying abuse and negative life experiences of Section 53 offenders in England and Wales.

What is also clear is that it is not simply minor delinquency or less severe offending which is explained by early background factors but also the more serious forms of offending behaviour. The problem this poses, at a time when there is considerable support for a more punitive approach to dealing with young offenders (see Asquith and Docherty, 1998), is that an evidence-based approach to preventing serious offending by children and young people would show that punitive measures fail to address the very factors which are known to contribute to serious offending in later life.

In many respects those young people who are perpetrators of the most serious forms of offending behaviour have themselves been the victims of equally damaging behaviours and relationships. This must surely have implications for a system of juvenile justice which emphasizes criminal responsibility and punishment for those convicted of the more serious offences, including murder.

We should also be aware that the literature is largely about boys, though Docherty (1997) does identify important differences in the nature of homicides committed by girls and boys. While our knowledge of the factors and circumstances thought to be highly significant in the lives of children who become violent is now more advanced, the most accurate predictor of violent behaviour is the sex of the child. There is a need to be careful, though, in developing explanatory frameworks which are gender sensitive. This again is supported by Boswell's work.

Boswell (1995) found that males made up 95% of children and young people sentenced under Section 53 of the Children and Young Persons Act 1933 in England and Wales. Given the importance of abuse and loss in these children's lives, she argues that abused males will externalize their reactions in the form of violent behaviour whereas girls will tend towards internalized responses in the form of psychiatric conditions including depression and self-harm. In discussing parricide, Docherty (1997) also identifies the much higher levels of murder of a parent by girls than by boys, boys being more likely to kill others.

What the work of Boswell also points to is the persistence of severe childhood antisocial behaviour into adolescence and the increased risk it represents for chronic delinquency. Disturbed young offenders who commit serious crimes may be amenable to prevention by means of early family support and education. Common among adolescents who murder is previous psychiatric contact, antisocial behaviour, history of substance abuse, mental illness within the family and marital conflict. She also noted that many of these children had been well known to a range of child agencies prior to admission.

The emphasis by Boswell, Docherty and those others reviewed briefly above on early life experiences serves to support the work of Farrington, who has argued that offending in general can be clearly explained in reference to negative experiences of children early in their lives. The thrust of Farrington's work (1994) is that the main implication of research on individual and family factors leading to offending by children is that early prevention should be the basis of any attempt to reduce the numbers of children at risk of becoming an offender. Strategies, whether punitively or welfare-based, are in many respects too late if they are applied only after the event. Developments in juvenile justice do in many instances derive from responses to cases (such as the Bulger case) and are often short term in objective.

Similarly, by implication, a system which emphasizes criminal responsibility and focuses on the offence will do little to prevent such behaviours and may well, by concentrating on what children have done, also fail to meet the needs of those offenders who can themselves be considered as victims. It is this principle which can be drawn from the work of Boswell and Bailey. Both illustrate the inappropriateness of a criminal justice system and penal measures which ignore the fundamental needs of children who have had horrific life experiences and who, in many instances, have been failed by major social institutions.

Two general points can be made here. One is that there is very little information in the UK on murder by children: the backgrounds of such children, the nature of their offences, what measures are applied and with what effect. The other, of course, is that if we are to develop a truly preventive strategy which is based on evidence then there has to be a political and indeed public mind shift to directing resources and a political will to address those factors known to put children at risk of becoming offenders.

Murder by children: principles for a preventive strategy

If the evidence of the current research literature were to be used as the basis for developing policies and practices for dealing with those children and young people who commit serious offences, a number of implications clearly follow. These provide the principles to be considered in the formulation of appropriate policies and practices.

Early intervention as the basis of a preventive strategy

On the basis of the work by Farrington, Boswell, Bailey and others referred to above, the causes of violent behaviour in children and young people are known and provide the basis for preventive strategies. Given the nature of the traumatic early-life experiences of children who commit serious offences, intervention in the lives of such children should be undertaken as early as possible. Farrington, throughout his work, has frequently spoken of the need for early intervention in the lives of children at risk of becoming offenders. What the research by Boswell and Bailey has done is to confirm Farrington's view that this applies equally to those who commit the more serious offences and that early intervention can have the added value of reducing the risk children face of exhibiting other behaviour problems later in life: 'Any measure which reduces crime will probably also reduce alcohol abuse, drink driving, drug abuse, sexual promiscuity, family violence, truancy, school failure, unemployment, marital disharmony and divorce. It is clear that problem children grow up into problem adults' (Farrington, 1994, p. 26).

Nor is the suggestion being made that the causes of serious violence can be attributed to parents or family life alone. It is clear that violence and other forms of offending are associated with such factors as poor parental discipline, marital and domestic disharmony, abuse, separation and loss, poverty, unemployment and disadvantage. But what all the research indicates is that it is not the presence of any one of these factors but rather a cluster of them which increases the risk that children will become offenders, and potentially serious offenders.

The merit of referring to offending trends in Central and Eastern Europe is that they clearly illustrate the impossibility of understanding the growth of delinquency and serious crime by the young without appreciating the significance of the wider social context. Similarly, the work of Farrington and that of Boswell point to the need for strategies which improve the life experiences generally of children who may be at risk and which may involve supporting families who are under particular stress because of poverty, disadvantage or other structural factors.

At least four inferences can be drawn from this. First, more information is needed on the nature of the life experiences of children who are at risk of becoming serious offenders. Second, more information is needed on available early intervention strategies which not only are successful but may have the potential to be successful in a

UK context. Strategies and measures successful in one social context may not necessarily graft readily into another. Third, resources for the prevention of serious offending by children and young people will have to be reallocated from tertiary prevention programmes and be targeted on the early life experiences of children. This was precisely the argument made in Childhood Matters, the Report of the National Commission of Inquiry into the Prevention of Child Abuse (whose members were greatly influenced by the work of Farrington): that there is a need for political will to transfer the considerable resources from measures dealing with those who have been abused to measures and strategies to prevent the abuse. Fourth is the importance of involving non-criminal justice agencies in the prevention of serious offending by children. The myth that criminal or juvenile justice systems alone will prevent offending by children can no longer be sustained. A truly preventive strategy is one which will address the life experiences of children and in which prevention will be promoted through the collaborative and integrated activities of a range of services.

We do know what the causes of serious offending are, and Farrington and others do provide a framework for developing preventive measures. Boswell and Bailey also clearly identify the factors in the backgrounds of those children who kill and these provide the basis for truly preventive strategies.

Children as perpetrators and children as victims

It is clear from the literature that those children who are at risk of becoming the more serious offenders and who inflict violence on others are themselves the victims of abuse and violence in their early childhoods. Though we have already referred to this above, the point is important enough to merit stating in its own right. Garbarino and Kostelny point to the inextricable relationship between those who are perpetrators and those who are victims. What they by implication also identify is that murder by children cannot simply be seen as a form of pathological or psychiatric disturbance but has to be seen in its wider social context.

The failure of punishment

There is considerable evidence indicating the failure of punitive measures to prevent offending by children and young people. There are, of course, other reasons for adopting a punitive approach but, given the back-grounds of those children and young people caught up in serious offending behaviour, the value of a punitive approach in preventing offending or reducing the risk that children might be involved in offending in later life has to be questioned.

What is even more worrying is that for some children their punishment may be harsher than that given to adults. The long-term effects on a child of such extended periods in detention are incalculable in terms of arrested social and emotional development. We urgently need to examine our response to children who commit serious violent offences, and how we can more effectively intervene at a much earlier stage in order to divert some children away from such a potentially catastrophic path.

As we have noted, the trends in juvenile offending clearly show that the majority of offenders commit less serious property offences and that only a few commit the more serious offences of violence and murder. Nevertheless, because of what we have referred to as 'twin tracking', the danger is that juvenile justice systems and crime control measures are disproportionately influenced by the need to deal with the more serious offender. The impact of the Bulger case on juvenile justice systems around Europe should not be underestimated.

On the basis of Farrington's work it can be argued that more punitive sentences are inappropriate for those who commit less serious offences. The argument here is that this applies equally to those children who commit the more serious offences and whose backgrounds manifest severe trauma.

Gender issues

Two comments can be made about the significance of gender in relation to serious offending. One is that international trends do suggest that young girls are increasingly involved in serious offending, though again the figures are still comparatively low. Nevertheless, there does appear to be an upward trend.

The second is that, from the work of Boswell, the way in which girls respond to the same kind of early-life experiences which propel boys into a serious offending career does appear to be different in that their behaviour is directed more at themselves and only rarely do they inflict violence on others. In Boswell's study, very few Section 53 offenders were girls, Docherty also identifies the different nature of killing by girls as compared to boys in terms of whom they kill.

There is a need for information on serious offending by children which is sensitive to gender (and other) issues in developing an explanatory framework. Further, given that most of the measures for dealing with serious offenders are designed to deal with boys, consideration must surely be given to examining their general relevance.

Age of criminal responsibility

The argument thus far has to be that a system which concentrates on the age of criminal responsibility, particularly in jurisdictions where the age of criminal responsibility is very low, may well fail children who themselves can be characterized as victims. The commitment to removing the principle of *doli incapax* (incapable of guilt) in England and Wales is evidence that far from seeking to raise the age of criminal responsibility, there is indeed a drive to hold more children criminally responsible for what they have done. The principle of *doli incapax* available in England and Wales for children between 10 and 13 implies that the prosecution must prove that the child knew the difference between right and wrong before a conviction can be secured. Such a shift must be taken in association with concerns expressed by others (Graham, 1996) about the way in which more and more young offenders are caught up in the criminal justice system.

Even in Central and Eastern Europe, where the age of criminal responsibility is higher (usually around 16 but may be lowered to 14 for the more serious offences), there is little support for the lowering of the age of criminal responsibility despite the rise in the number of serious offences committed by children and young people. What we also know from the work of Dunkel (1991) in reviewing criminal and juvenile justice systems throughout Europe is that in those countries which have raised their age of criminal responsibility there have been no discernible negative effects in terms of increase in crime.

The age of criminal responsibility in the UK has to be addressed in the light of the evidence from such literature as exists in the UK and the wider international arena. And as argued above, examining the principles on which the age of criminal responsibility is based also has important implications for the very philosophy of juvenile justice systems.

Prevention: the allocation of resources

The development of preventive strategies has historically, in a number of social welfare fields, been inhibited by the lack of available resources. And as was noted by the National Commission on the Prevention of Child Abuse in the report *Childhood Matters* (1996), it could be cost-effective to reallocate resources and funds to early intervention strategies with subsequent savings resulting from the reduced numbers of children dealt with when they reach their teens. This does, of course, require political will and a radical rethinking of policies and practices for dealing with those who commit the more serious offences.

Rights for children

Children's rights have become increasingly important on the political
agenda, and, with the ratification by the UK of the United Nations
Convention on the Rights of the Child, all child law is to be based on
principles drawn from that convention. Debate about rights for children
in the context of juvenile justice systems has usually been about the way in
which children's rights are denied within systems of juvenile justice. It is
appropriate, then, that changes be made to the internal workings of
juvenile justice systems to ensure that children have access to fundamental
rights such as the right to be heard, the right to a fair hearing, the right to
representation and so on. However, the UN Convention on the Rights of
the Child also promotes the right of children, of all children, to be
provided with the resources, support and wherewithal for healthy growth
and development. This of course fits neatly with a philosophy which
explains offending behaviour by reference to the nature of the negative life
experiences of children. What it also promotes – and this is the line taken
in Childhood Matters – is the principle that in order to reduce the risk
some children face of becoming an offender, the best strategy is to
promote positive life experiences for all children. This has significant
implications for our argument here.

Programmes and measures for dealing with or seeking to prevent
delinquency or offending have to be part of a much wider consideration of
how justly life chances are distributed to our children. Justice for children
who commit offences cannot simply be about their just treatment within
legal or formal systems of control – important though that may be. It has
to be about the way life chances and opportunities are provided equally
for all children. That is precisely the principle on which the UN
Convention on the Rights of the Child is based: that all children have the
right to experience those conditions and circumstances which can best
contribute to healthy growth and development. The historical failure of
traditional juvenile justice systems to substantially reduce or prevent
offending by children and young people can largely be attributed to the
fact that intervention is often too late and does not tackle the real
problems. We can no longer perpetuate the myth that our current systems
of justice for children are in truth able to tackle the problem, or indeed
that the problem is simply offending behaviour – that is, blaming the
victim.

Policies for dealing with those who commit the most serious offences
will ultimately fail if they are premised upon the centrality of criminal
responsibility and punishment. The historical failure of juvenile justice
systems in general to prevent offending crystallizes the need for a
fundamental review of the principles on which they are based. A concern
with how we deal with children who commit the most serious acts leads to

a fundamental appraisal of the way in which we as adults relate to children generally; the assumptions about childhood and children embedded in our most cherished institutions; and the very status given to children in society. The 'angel' or 'devil' dichotomy is an impoverished perspective from which to develop our reactions and responses to what children do – no matter how serious their acts.

References

Asquith, S. (1992) *Evolution of Juvenile Delinquency in Western Europe.* Strasbourg: Council of Europe.

Asquith, S. (ed.) (1996) *Juvenile Justice in Central and Eastern Europe.* Strasbourg: Council of Europe.

Asquith, S. (1998) Children's hearings in an international context. In A. Lockyer and F. Stone (eds), *Juvenile Justice in Scotland*, pp. 238–52. Edinburgh: T. &T. Clarke.

Asquith, S. and Docherty, M. (1998) Preventing offending by children and young people in Scotland. In P. Duff and N. Hutton (eds), *Criminal Justice in Scotland*, pp. 243–61 Aldershot: Dartmouth Publishing.

Bailleau, F. (1996) Social crime prevention: juvenile delinquency. In S. Asquith (ed.), *Children and Young People in Conflict with the Law*, pp. 43–55. London: Jessica Kingsley.

Boswell, G. (1995) Violent victims: the prevalence of abuse and loss in the lives of Section 53 offenders. London: The Prince's Trust.

Cavadino, P. (ed.) (1996) *Children Who Kill.* London: British Juvenile and Family Courts Magistrates Association.

Childhood Matters (1996) Report of the National Commission of Inquiry into the Prevention of Child Abuse. London: The Stationery Office.

Children and Violence (1995) Report of the Gulbenkian Commission on Children and Violence, London.

Docherty, M. (1997) Parricide: a review of literature on children who kill. Centre for the Child and Society, University of Glasgow.

Dunkel, F. (1991) Legal differences in criminology in Europe. In T. Booth (ed.), *Juvenile Justice in the New Europe* Sheffield: Social Services Monograph.

Farrington, D. (1994) Early developmental prevention of juvenile delinquency, *Journal of the Royal Society for the Promotion of the Arts and Commerce*, November, 22–34.

Garbarino, J. and Kostelny, K. (1996) Children and violence: trauma and the American war zone. In S. Asquith (ed.), *Children and Young People in Conflict with the Law*, pp. 92–101. London: Jessica Kingsley.

Graham, J. (1996) The organization and functioning of juvenile justice in England and Wales. In S. Asquith (ed.), *Children and Young People in Conflict with the Law*, pp. 73–91. London: Jessica Kingsley.

Thornberry, T. (1994) quoted in editorial, *Carnegie Quarterly*, 39 (Winter), 4.

Walgrave, L. (1996) Restorative juvenile justice: a way to restore justice in Western European systems. In S. Asquith (ed.), *Children and Young People in Conflict with the Law*, pp. 169–99. London: Jessica Kingsley.

Wilson, J. and Howell, J. (1995) Comprehensive strategy for serious, violent and chronic juvenile offenders. In J. Howell, B. Krisberg, D. Hawkins and J. Wilson (eds), *Serious, Violent and Chronic Juvenile Offenders*, London: Sage.

9

Government for children

Peter Newell

It should be evident to any government that children, both as children and as the future of society, justify a high priority. It should also be transparently clear to any government that it ignores children at its peril. Common sense, backed by overwhelming research evidence, tells us that the economic and social costs of neglecting children and failing to promote their positive development are very high indeed.

Just as neglect and insensitive treatment of the environment put the planet's future at risk, so it is with children. What happens to children in the early years within the family and school, and even in the womb, significantly determines their growth and development. Their cost or contribution to society will be spread over the rest of their lives.

Why do children deserve special treatment?

Citizens deserve a government sensitive to their needs. What then is so special about children? First, their healthy development and active participation are uniquely crucial to the future of human society. Children begin their lives totally dependent on adults and grow towards independence only with the help of adults. During this developmental stage they are particularly vulnerable to the actions and inactions of adults and governments. They are disproportionately affected by poverty, poor housing, environmental pollution. At the same time, almost every area of government policy affects children either directly or indirectly, and indeed many policies are targeted exclusively at children. Education services dominate huge chunks of childhood; public health policies target their developing bodies and lifestyles. Child protection is a substantial professional industry.

What is more, some of the most significant current society-wide changes – to family structures and employment patterns, and the domination of market forces, now even in public services – affect children disproportionately.

And children, unlike the rest of us, can play no significant part in the political process. They have no vote or direct political power. While in many countries (including the UK) there are the beginnings of attempts to consult children about some sorts of decisions and local services, such initiatives are neither common nor consistent. Children's views barely permeate central government. A British Youth Council survey in 1995 found that of the 5000 names in the Cabinet Office central list of people recommended for seats on 'non-departmental public bodies', only 5 per cent were under 40, and the average age was 55 (British Youth Council, 1995).

Suggesting that children's interests should be represented at the heart of government is not new. In the UK, proposals for a Minister for Children first surfaced in the 1970s (Jackson, 1976). In 1976 the Court Committee on child health services in its report 'Fit for the future' proposed the formation of a Children's Committee, to be a joint committee of the Central Health Services Council and the Personal Social Services Council, two existing government advisory bodies. Established in 1978, the Children's Committee was the first attempt at a governmental body for children. It had a short life, killed off in 1981 under the new government's policy of retaining only those non-departmental public bodies which were 'clearly essential'; the Secretary of State 'did not consider the Children's Committee passed this test' (Department of Health and Social Security, 1981).

In one of its final reports, 'The representation of children's rights and interests' (Children's Committee, 1981), the Committee discussed various proposed initiatives including a Minister for Children, an Inter-Departmental Advisory Council, a Children's Ombudsperson (Norway had appointed the world's first during that year) and a Children's Commission or Council, 'standing apart from government but relating closely to it'. These proposals were kept alive by various committees and publications during the 1980s, but there was no enthusiasm from government. In 1991 the Calouste Gulbenkian Foundation commissioned a feasibility study of the proposal for a children's rights commissioner for the UK, published as 'Taking children seriously' (Rosenbaum and Newell, 1996). The proposal has been widely supported by non-governmental organizations and local government associations. The Labour Party was persuaded to include proposals for both a Minister for Children and an independent Children's Rights Commissioner in its manifesto for the 1992 general election. By 1997 more than 80 national organizations, including four Royal Colleges of Health, were promoting the idea of a commissioner, but neither it nor the Minister for Children found a place in that year's Labour Party manifesto.

It was in the run-up to the 1997 election that the Calouste Gulbenkian Foundation commissioned a unique inquiry into effective government structures for children, publishing a report with detailed recommendations

(Hodgkin and Newell, 1996). The inquiry focused on central government, and surveyed both current arrangements and responsibilities for children across government and the views of organizations and individuals working with and for children on how government was serving children's interests. But before I detail the results of the inquiry and the report's recommendations for improving government for children, it is important to consider the international scene.

The Convention on the Rights of the Child

As part of the Gulbenkian Foundation initiative, UNICEF collaborated in an international survey designed to provide snapshots of governmental arrangements for children in states across the world. Internationally, there has been a flurry of activity provoked by the United Nations Convention on the Rights of the Child (CRC). The Convention, adopted by the General Assembly in 1989, has become in less than a decade the most widely accepted of human rights instruments. It has been ratified by 192 states, leaving only the children of Somalia (a country with no effective government) and those of the United States (a country which should know better, but exhibits a staggeringly hypocritical attitude to human rights) outside the CRC's protection. As well as promoting the human rights of children, the Convention has also had a knock-on effect on the ratification of other key international treaties.

The CRC got off to a good start thanks to the World Summit for Children in September 1990, when 71 heads of state and government gathered in New York and pledged: 'The well-being of children requires political action at the highest level. We are determined to take that action. We ourselves make a solemn commitment to give high priority to the rights of children.' It is wise to maintain some cynicism about the effects on children's lives of such symbolic commitments; this one was made at a meeting whose attendance rate owed more to the then imminent crisis in the Gulf than to empathy with children's rights. A common reaction to the Convention is 'Just another piece of paper. Look at the horror of children's lives – and deaths – in many of the countries which have signed up.'

It is true that the Convention is not enforceable in the way the European Human Rights Convention is: individual children cannot take cases to a court. But the process of reporting by states and monitoring by an independent elected committee of experts (the Committee on the Rights of the Child) which the Convention has established, has surprised many by its ability to provoke first an analysis of children's situations, and then action. At an international level UNICEF (whose mission since 1996 has been guided by the convention, striving 'to establish children's rights as enduring ethical principles and international standards of behaviour towards children') and other UN agencies have kept up the pressure, and at national level there has been a rapid, linked expansion in the number and influence of non-governmental organizations working for the human rights of children.

'General measures' for implementing the Convention

The Committee on the Rights of the Child has from the beginning underlined the importance of governments' developing distinctive structures to ensure sensitivity to children. The ten members, elected by states which have ratified, have been particularly innovative in developing guidance for governments on what they have termed 'general measures of implementation'. The Convention requires each state to prepare a detailed report on progress towards implementation, an 'initial report' within two years of ratification, and then periodic reports every five years thereafter. (For a detailed account of the reporting process under the convention, together with the developing interpretation of each of the Convention's 42 substantive articles, see UNICEF, 1998.) It is in the very detailed guidelines for reporting that the committee has set out its definition of these 'general measures' (Committee on the Rights of the Child, 1991a, b). They include:

- development of a comprehensive national strategy for children;
- development of effective co-ordination of policies and actions for children;
- development of one or more permanent government mechanisms for children, to promote co-ordination, implementation and systematic monitoring;
- comprehensive and ongoing review of all legislation to ensure compatibility with the Convention, and to ensure children have a remedy when their rights are violated;
- measures to ensure implementation of economic, social and cultural rights to the maximum extent of available resources (including necessary budgetary analysis, etc.) and use of international co-operation to foster implementation;
- development of arrangements to ensure adequate child impact analysis during policy formulation and decision-making at all levels of government in all departments;
- development of independent statutory offices for children – children's ombudspeople or commissioners;
- sufficient data collection on the state of children;

- development of co-operation to implement the Convention between government and civil society, including non-governmental organizations and children;
- dissemination of the Convention to make its principles and provisions widely known to adults and children;
- development of training concerning the Convention for all those involved in government for children, and who work with or for children;
- dissemination of reports under the Convention to make them widely available to the public.

The Convention states a general obligation 'to undertake all appropriate legislative, administrative and other measures for the implementation of the rights recognised in the present Convention' (Article 4). This is supplemented by the non-discrimination principle in Article 2: 'to respect and ensure the rights set forth in the present Convention to each child within their jurisdiction without discrimination of any kind'. There is also a 'safety net' principle: the state must 'ensure the child such protection and care as is necessary for his or her well-being', respecting the rights and duties of parents and others legally responsible (Article 3). Another important general obligation is 'to make the principles and provisions of the Convention widely known, by appropriate and active means, to adults and children alike' (Article 42). Reporting and the obligation to make reports widely available to the public are set out in Article 44.

When the Committee was examining Canada's initial report in 1995, a member commented that, given the wide range of administrative and legislative systems among ratifying states, the Committee was in no position to specify particular solutions:

> Indeed, a degree of diversity in the mechanisms set up to implement the Convention might lead to a degree of competition, which could be very beneficial. The important point was that the Convention should be the main benchmark and inspiration of action at the provincial and central level. (Committee on the Rights of the Child, 1995a)

If we look at least superficially at governments around the world, it seems that the hoped-for competition may be developing: the international survey carried out in 1996 with UNICEF help found that most states had established some mechanism close to the centre of government with a co-ordinating responsibility for children: a National Commission, National Council for Children headed by the Prime Minister, Higher Council for Childhood chaired by the Minister for Social Affairs, Co-ordinating Council for Youth and Children's Affairs within the Prime Minister's Office, a Cabinet Office Unit, Minister for Children, Inter-Ministerial

Committee for Children. Many states annually publish and debate in their parliaments 'State of Children' reports. Some are planning, if not yet applying, child impact analysis. At least three – Norway, Sweden and South Africa – have published 'children's budgets'. A sign of even greater commitment to children and a willingness to be held accountable to that commitment is the establishment by many governments of independent offices for children – children's ombudspeople or commissioners for children.

The Committee on the Rights of the Child has already examined over 70 initial reports from states in all continents. In each case it reviews the state's report; invites UNICEF and other international bodies and also national NGOs to submit comments and to meet the committee; asks the state for further information; and then meets with government representatives to examine progress towards implementation. This examination of each report normally covers three 3-hour sessions in the Palais des Nations in Geneva. The Committee invariably spends some time questioning whether there are distinctive structures for children in government, sufficient signs of co-ordination across the major departments, a comprehensive review of legislation, and so on. The Committee's 'concluding observations', produced after the examination, follow a standard format: positive aspects, then factors and difficulties impeding implementation, principal subjects for concern, and finally suggestions and recommendations. A recurring theme in a majority of the concluding observations is the need to develop special structures and to co-ordinate policies for children more effectively.

The Committee on the Rights of the Child: comments on the UK

The Committee's concluding observations on the UK, prepared following examination of the initial UK report in January 1995, included the following:

> The Committee remains unclear about the extent to which an effective co-ordinating mechanism exists for the implementation of the Convention on the Rights of the Child. It is concerned whether sufficient consideration has been given to the establishment of mechanisms, including of an independent nature, to co-ordinate and monitor the implementation of the rights of the child.

The committee went on to propose

> that the State party consider establishing a national mechanism for the purpose of co-ordinating the implementation of the Convention, including between government departments and between central and local governmental authorities. Furthermore the Committee suggests that the State party establish

a permanent mechanism for the monitoring of the Children's Act and the Convention on the Rights of the Child throughout the United Kingdom. (Committee on the Rights of the Child, 1995b)

The significance of the process of reporting and the examination of states' reports by the Committee on the Rights of the Child is that it is the only external accountability that states and their governments face for the way they treat their children. It is a process with huge potential for improving the status of children; it creates a new worldwide political priority for children and thus in time should immeasurably improve the quality of human societies.

The European Strategy for Children

At a regional level, the Parliamentary Assembly of the Council of Europe adopted the European Strategy for Children on 24 January 1996, reflecting developments under the Convention and the work of the Committee on the Rights of the Child. The strategy commends member states to 'make children's rights a political priority' and proposes a series of steps to reflect and promote this priority:

i) adopting at national and local level a pro-active childhood policy which seeks full implementation of the Convention on the Rights of the Child, which will consider the best interests of the child as a guiding principle of all action and which will anticipate situations instead of trying to deal with emergencies or problems that have already arisen;

ii) making children more visible through the systematic collection of information, in particular reliable, detailed (by age and gender), comparable statistics which will make it possible to identify their needs and the issues which require priority political action;

iii) adopting a comprehensive, consistent and co-ordinated approach to childhood policy, which will encourage multi-disciplinary structures to be put in place at all deliberation and decision-making levels, in particular at ministerial level, and foster the creation of national coalitions of all relevant partners;

iv) appointing a commissioner (ombudsperson) for children or another structure offering guarantees of independence, and the responsibilities required to improve children's lives, and accessible to the public through such means as local offices;

v) ensuring, especially at policy-making level, that the interests and needs of children are always duly considered and taken into account, for example by introducing practices such as the 'child impact statement' which offers a way of determining the probable impact on children of any proposed legislative, regulatory or other measures in whatever field, for example, in the field of legal aid;

vi)   investing in children and giving them budgetary priority by allocating
adequate and fair resources in relation to spending on the needs of the
other sections of the population at all levels (national, regional, local).
(Recommendations to the Committee of Ministers, 1996)

UK: Inquiry into Effective Government Structures for Children

It was against this backdrop of international and European developments
for children that the Inquiry into Effective Government Structures for
Children started work in the UK in 1995, seeking to identify the aims of
government for children and proposing the following:

- to ensure the healthy and happy development of children to their full
potential, both as children now, and for the future well-being of
society;
- to encourage the active, responsible participation of children in society,
enabling them to grow into responsible adults;
- to acknowledge the diversity of children – including age, geographical
location, cultural and ethnic background, abilities and aspirations;
- to fulfil and develop the spirit as well as the letter of existing domestic
children's legislation in all jurisdictions;
- to meet international obligations to make children a high political
priority and to implement fully the UN Convention on the Rights of the
Child;
- to make the best use of inevitably limited resources.

The inquiry went on to identify various failings of government in the UK.
First, it found a failure to give children any overt political priority; one has
only to look at the variety of initiatives in other countries which have
developed with the authority of presidents or prime ministers or cabinets
to see what is possible. In the UK, the focus on children in government
remains very largely on bad children, on demonizing children, on children
as objects of concern.

Next, there is the invisibility of children in government. Effective
policies require a detailed understanding of the current position, what
children's needs are and how they can be met. At present there is no
annual report on the state of children in the UK, no systematic collection
of statistics on all aspects of children's lives, no requirement to assess and
publish information on the potential and actual impact of government
policies on children, no analysis of overall or departmental budgets to
assess the proportion spent on children or the proportion spent on
'preventive' rather than responsive 'crisis' services.

But it is inadequate co-ordination that most concerns those working with children. Respondents identified some positive examples, including the growth of children's services planning within local government, and joint guidance and training seminars on the implementation of some policies which cross departmental boundaries. But the overwhelming message was of the serious problems caused to children by lack of co-ordination at central government level. Examples given covered broad issues including funding: different departments do not co-ordinate the funding of initiatives by statutory and voluntary agencies despite big overlaps of aims. The result is reduced flexibility in providing the most cost-effective delivery. Departments tend to commission research within their areas of responsibility, often leading to a blinkered understanding of the children's issues which float across or between these responsibilities. There was a long list of specific policy issues for which lack of co-ordination caused identified problems: responding to special educational needs, child protection, young offenders and crime prevention, early-years care and education, homelessness of young people, children in poor or temporary housing, family law and courts issues, refugee children.

Professor John Stewart of the Institute of Local Government Studies at the University of Birmingham coined the phrase 'the wicked issues' to describe intractably complicated issues with certain common characteristics: first, an issue not fully understood, neither the nature of the problem nor its solution; second, an issue involving more than one department and not being dealt with satisfactorily by any. Wicked issues are often found to be the unintended consequence of some other policy objective, arising because of a failure to look at the matter holistically. Professor Stewart's first list of 'wicked issues' included the environment, community safety and discrimination.

Many child-related topics conform to the definition of a wicked issue. School exclusions is one example. Expulsions have trebled in England and Wales between 1990 and 1994/95. The reasons are not fully understood, and different parties to the problem identify different causes: the introduction of market forces and competition between schools, inappropriateness of the National Curriculum, failure to identify special educational needs, failure of parental discipline, too many controls on headteachers' powers, oversize classes and restricted resources.

The problem belongs to more than one department: the Department for Education and Employment for obvious reasons, but also for less obvious ones: the relationship between a decrease in funding and provision of community youth services, and disruptive behaviour; the Home Office because of the identified link between exclusion and the onset of offending; the Department of Health in terms of both physical and mental health needs; social services because most excluded children conform to the definition of children in need, and a disproportionate number of them are children in public care whose parents are often in need of support. The solution cannot lie with one department alone.

Of course there are attempts at interdepartmental co-ordination and co-operation over some of these issues (including some welcome new initiatives such as the Social Exclusion Unit (see p. 173)). But focusing co-ordination on wicked issues tends to over-pathologize the issues, to adopt a tunnel vision perspective which misses the real solution because the problem is perceived exclusively as the troublesome child, rather than as a network involving the child, the family, the professional system and the underpinning policies. In particular, it is likely to focus on first aid rather than prevention, on ambulances at the bottom of the cliff rather than fences at the top.

Linked both to the invisibility of children in budgeting and to lack of co-ordination is the inefficient use of resources in central government. Prevention, almost by definition, is a multi-agency affair. Moves towards integrated funding to promote shared goals at local level can too often, according to those in local authorities who should know, be inhibited by functional stratification, policy differences and crude rivalries between central government departments.

There is no government strategy, and no government department, to champion the responsible participation of children in society. Instead, we have accumulating evidence of the alienation of children and young people from politics and the 'democratic process' which so comprehensively excludes them. When children are given greater responsibilities – in the family, in schools, in neighbourhood and community projects – the well-documented benefits accrue.

Arising from the analysis from a children's perspective of what is wrong with government, and from the identified overall aims of government for children, the report 'Effective government structures for children' (Hodgkin and Newell, 1996) produces a preliminary list of detailed functions:

- to ensure that there is an overall UK-wide governmental strategy for children, based on appropriate principles. (The UN Convention on the Rights of the Child provides the obvious foundation of principles and standards. In 1996 the then government identified the Convention as a foundation for local planning of children's services.);
- to make children, and the direct and indirect effects of policies on children, more visible in government;
- to ensure that children's needs are addressed adequately and systematically throughout government;
- to ensure effective co-ordination of planning and policy development across government and between its various levels;

- to promote children's active participation in society by consulting them, taking their views into account, and recognizing their evolving capacities to play a responsible part in decision-making in services and institutions, in neighbourhoods and local communities, and in local and national political processes.

The report goes on to propose new government structures. While it makes specific proposals, it recognizes the need to look for pragmatic ways of developing existing structures. First, it underlines that without commitment from the highest level, including the support of the prime minister, new structures are unlikely to have real impact. A large majority of respondents favoured appointment of a Minister for Children, but most raised reservations. A weak post could marginalize rather than promote children as a priority (bad experiences with ministers for disabled people and for women were cited). If the minister is situated in one of the major functional departments, this could allow other departments to abdicate responsibilities for children. The idea of establishing a comprehensive 'children's department' carving major responsibilities out of other departments was rejected as not feasible for the moment, but worth detailed study including the examination of related models in other countries.

In summary, the report, which pre-dated devolution of powers to Northern Ireland, Scotland and Wales, proposes:

- within the Prime Minister's Office: appropriate advisers with acknowledged expertise on children;
- in Cabinet: a senior cabinet minister with responsibility for children (probably along with other responsibilities); within current constitutional arrangements the Secretaries of State for Northern Ireland, Scotland and Wales would add the perspective of the children in these countries to cabinet deliberations;
- a minister of state, designated Minister for Children, sited in the Cabinet Office and having responsibility for a Cabinet Office Children's Unit;
- junior ministers with responsibility for children in the Northern Ireland, Scottish and Welsh Offices, reporting to the Secretaries of State, and with a senior official in each office to ensure co-ordination between the various departments. (The report included detailed sections on government structures in Northern Ireland, Scotland and Wales, and some discussion of proposed constitutional changes and devolution.);
- a cabinet committee, or subcommittee, on children, or a Standing Inter-Ministerial Group on Children, with a 'shadow' group of senior officials.

In Parliament, the report proposes a special-focus Select Committee on Children in the House of Commons. Outside government, the report lends its support to the proposal for an independent Children's Rights Commissioner, with separate but linked commissioners for England, Northern Ireland, Scotland and Wales.

So what are the functions of the proposed Minister for Children, supported by the Cabinet Office Children's Unit? These could be UK-wide, in collaboration with the nominated ministers in Scotland, Wales and Northern Ireland, or directly on behalf of children in England:

- drawing up the governmental strategy for UK children, for approval by cabinet;
- servicing the cabinet committee or subcommittee or standing inter-ministerial committee on children and other co-ordinating committees or *ad hoc* groups on specific children's issues, and securing other forms of interdepartmental co-ordination;
- analysing the impact of government policy on children;
- reporting annually to Parliament on the current state of children in the UK and progress towards meeting the objectives identified in the Strategy for Children;
- encouraging and facilitating integrated funding between departments and agencies to secure particular outcomes for children;
- taking on responsibility for progressing overarching legislation relating to children;
- developing pilot mechanisms for listening and responding to the concerns of children and young people, and for giving them more civic responsibility;
- making proposals as necessary for transfer of or changes to specified responsibilities for children between departments, and identifying and initiating new mechanisms for securing joint responsibility in certain areas;
- overseeing and developing joint planning for children's services at a local level.

There has been separate promotion in the UK of the idea of a Minister for the Family, or for 'Youth'. These are emphatically rejected by the report. It defines 'children' as the UN Convention on the Rights of the Child does, as everyone under 18 years of age – a distinct group with a common set of needs arising from their state of dependency, evolving capacities and disenfranchisement. Of course the needs, rights and responsibilities of children are inextricably bound up with the needs, rights and responsibilities of their families and particularly their parents. But definitions of 'the family' and 'youth' are often so wide as to be meaningless. And while there is overlap between the three groups' interests, recognition of children's distinct circumstances can become lost or blurred if considered only in a family context. Parents are usually children's first and best advocates, but may also be the source of many of their problems, and on occasion parents can be children's first and worst enemies.

The purpose of the focus on children is not to downgrade in any way the importance of adult family members, or of young adults, but to develop structures which ensure that relevant aspects of family and youth policy are sensitive to children. The youth lobby tends to be dominated by the interests of the older age-range, and 'the family' can be used to promote policies which are inimical to children.

Progress towards child-sensitive government

At the time of writing, it is now over two years since 'Effective government structures for children' (Hodgkin and Newell, 1996) was published. At the time of its launch, the National Society for the Prevention of Cruelty to Children (NSPCC) commissioned an opinion poll, which found that more than two-thirds of a representative sample of adults (and 77 per cent of those who were parents) thought that politicians gave 'little thought' to the effects of their policies on children, with just 4 per cent believing they gave 'a lot' of thought. Eighty per cent supported the proposal for a Minister for Children (with greater support from parents and from younger age groups).

It is also over two years since the new Labour government took office, in May 1997. This is a government which has indicated an overall concern to improve cross-departmental co-ordination. But for children, as yet there is little sign of a co-ordinated new focus. No UK-wide Governmental Strategy for Children. No Minister for Children in Whitehall. No cabinet-level initiative. But there have been some related developments and, perhaps most important, a new openness to debate old and new ideas.

Some innovations in Whitehall (for example the Social Exclusion Unit) do cover some children's issues (school exclusions and looked-after children in particular) but have no particular children's perspective. And the nearest thing we have in England to a Minister for Children – the Parliamentary Under-Secretary of State in the Department of Health, who is responsible for children's services along with a long list of other major responsibilities – has announced a review of the proposal for a children's commissioner, including an evaluation of similar offices for children in other countries. So this proposal, popular throughout the children's world, is now receiving serious consideration.

The same junior minister in the Department of Health has been given the task of co-ordinating preparation of the second UK report under the

Convention on the Rights of the Child. The first report was prepared with minimal involvement of non-governmental organizations, patchy reporting across government and grossly inadequate coverage of developments in Northern Ireland, Scotland and Wales. This time the process has started well with a broad consultative conference, an advisory group with NGO representatives, and detailed questionnaires circulated widely within and outside government.

Both Scotland and Wales have now nominated Ministers for Children's Issues (albeit with many other responsibilities). In Wales the Minister is served by a 'Children and Families Unit' in the Welsh Office. In Scotland the Minister has announced a system for 'child-proofing' new policies, including development of a Child Care Strategy Statement to ensure that the effects of relevant policy development on children are fully taken into account.

Some of the most radical ideas about government for children (not as of February 1998 leading to action) are emanating from the Treasury. As part of the current Comprehensive Spending Reviews, a Cross-Departmental Review of Provision for Young Children (under-8s) is being conducted, with a ministerial advisory board. This is promoting preventive policies, and highlighting the lack of comprehensive information about children and about the money currently spent on them, the lack of government-wide co-ordination across the whole spectrum of services for young children, and the lack of any agreed government-wide objectives for young children. It looks as though the resulting reports may strongly advocate new structures as well as new means of resource allocation and service delivery to children locally.

So there are some glimmers of hope, and in the non-governmental sector there are energetic advocates for children who will continue to press government to take children seriously. But what is sad, and serious too, is that there is so little sign of leaders in the UK seeing the point of focusing government effectively and positively on children, seeing how much there is to gain by doing so. Instead, the tendency to demonize and blame children persists, led by sections of the media and unchallenged by government. It is not just children who are the losers.

Peter Newell is the co-author with Rachel Hodgkin of 'Effective government structures for children', published by the Gulbenkian Foundation, London, 1996. Free summaries of the report are available from the Foundation, 98 Portland Place, London W1N 4ET. The complete report is available from Turnaround Publisher Services Ltd, Unit 3, Olympia Trading Estate, Coburg Road, Wood Green, London N22 6TZ. Price £10.95.

References

British Youth Council (1995) Young people, politics and voting. London: BYC.

Children's Committee (1981) The representation of children's rights and interests. London: HMSO.

Committee on the Rights of the Child (1991a) General guidelines regarding the form and contents of initial reports to be submitted by States Parties. CRC/C/5.

Committee on the Rights of the Child (1991b) General guidelines regarding the form and contents of periodic reports to be submitted by States Parties. CRC/C/58.

Committee on the Rights of the Child (1995a) Summary report of discussions between Committee on the Rights of the Child and Canadian Government representatives. CRC/C/SR.214.

Committee on the Rights of the Child (1995b) Concluding observations of the Committee on the Rights of the Child: United Kingdom of Great Britain and Northern Ireland. CRC/C/15/Add.34.

Court Report (1976) Fit for the future: report of the Committee on Child Health Services (chairperson: Donald Court). London: HMSO.

Department of Health and Social Security (1981) Press release, 11 June.

Hodgkin, R. and Newell, P. (1996) Effective government structures for children: report of a Gulbenkian Foundation inquiry. London: Gulbenkian Foundation.

Jackson, B. (1976) A Minister for Children. *New Society*, 15 January.

Recommendations to the Committee of Ministers of the Council of Europe (1996) In Report on a European Strategy for Children adopted by the Parliamentary Assembly of the Council of Europe.

Rosenbaum, M. and Newell, P. (1991) Taking children seriously: a proposal for a Children's Rights Commissioner. London: Calouste Gulbenkian Foundation.

Stewart, J. (1995) *Local Government Today: An Observer's View*. Local Management Board.

UNICEF (1998) *Implementation Handbook for the Rights of the Child*. New York: UNICEF.

Willow, C. (1997) Hear! Hear! Promoting children's and young people's democratic participation in local government. London: Local Government Information Unit in association with National Children's Bureau and Children's Rights Office.

World Summit for Children (1990) World declaration on the survival, protection and development of children. New York: UN.

Index

Children and the State: Whose Problem?